3D WORLD

presents

Luis Arizaga

For our animation special this issue we could think of few artists better qualified to evoke the movement of the medium than Luis Arizaga. The CEO and creative director of Digital Rebel Studio in Barcelona created his dynamic cover image in his spare time using Blender and Gimp.

Luis tries to find techniques or methods that are easy to adapt to any software, and has been looking at ways to create fast 3D prototypes of his models. He uses a combination of poly modelling to control topology and digital sculpting to add details. The artist particularly enjoyed two stages in the creative process: designing and sculpting the character. He likes getting real-time feedback from his image, and also being able to pose the character or add an expression in just a few minutes.

Luis has recently started Digital Rebel Academy, a digital art school where he teaches students how to create high-quality 3D characters. A good education can give you a big head start in the CG industry, so turn to page 37 for our guide to the best animation schools and advice on how to secure your place.
digital-rebel.com

A wireframe of Luis Arizaga's Captain Proton, which appears on this issue's cover

Lightwave™ ELEVEN

Take Your Art to the Brink of Reality

The latest version of NewTek LightWave™ 3D animation software takes your art to the edge.
A complete palette of tools, LightWave 11 is professional, faster and way more powerful.
TV. Film. Architectural visualization. Print. And Game development. Get incredible detail.
Instancing. Flocking motion. Fracture. Bullet Dynamics. Virtual Studio Tools. HyperVoxels™
Blending. GoZ™ technology. Freedom to stretch your imagination. For real.

NewTek
LightWave 11

Five things you'll find in every issue of 3D World

Expert analysis and opinion

1 Get under the skin of the 3D industry with regular assessments of industry trends. Pre-Viz looks at what's happening right now, while Post-Production and our in-depth features offer privileged access to the biggest names in the industry as they share their expertise with you.

Road-tested tutorials

2 Seasoned professionals from across the 3D industry write tutorials based on projects created especially for you. We test every step ourselves to ensure accuracy and accessibility.

Inspiring artwork

3 We comb all areas of the 3D scene to find the best examples of work that's being produced today, from the hottest commercials to game cinematics and illustrations. 3D World reflects the state of the art every month.

The whole of the 3D scene

4 Why restrict yourself? Whatever your main creative discipline, 3D World enables you to keep up with trends and techniques across animation, visual effects, games illustration and architecture. As the world of 3D evolves, so does 3D World.

Free disc

5 **Your free disc contains 3D resources with an average commercial value of $249.** Every month you'll receive a disc crammed with the best 3D assets we can lay our hands on, including the scene files you need to complete our training projects.

Welcome to 3D WORLD

Learn from animators of the past, and shape animation's future

Forget all of the tools that today's 3D animation software offers. Forget about the hard-surface modelling, retopologising, UV-mapping, ambient occlusion and 1,001 other technologies that enables your software to achive such wonderful, true-to-life results.

Ultimately, great animation depends on what's it's always been about: observation and interpretation. Whether you're capturing your interpretation of life through a pencil and tracing paper or Maya really isn't that important. That's why you should never ignore the lessons you can learn from the great animators of the past: collectively, they've already figured out the hardest parts of animation, and they've been generous enough to pass that knowledge down the generations.

The 12 principles developed during the classic era of Walt Disney animation and published by Frank Thomas and Ollie Johnston should be pinned up next to every animator's workstation: they're a reminder of the building blocks that breathe life into your work, turning craft into art. We recap those guidelines on page 28, with visual examples from some of the best animation shorts of recent times, plus further advice from some of today's best animators.

Our animation focus this issue blossoms with a giant guide to 20 of the world's best animation schools: still the best way to hone your craft, despite the undoubted benefits of training DVDs, books and (ahem) magazine tutorials. Tour these faculties and discover what it takes to secure your place on page 37.

Wanted: your feedback

We're always looking to take 3D World forward, and we'd like to know what you want to see. Whether it's the magazine, 3dworldmag.com, our digital editions or even our Twitter feed, we welcome your suggestions for what you'd like to see and where you think we could do better. My email address is richard.hill@futurenet.com.

Richard Hill, editor

SUBSCRIBERS
Got a question about your 3D World subscription? Email 3dworld@myfavouritemagazines.co.uk

---

Contact 3D World

General enquiries
Richard Hill
Editor
01225 442244
richard.hill@futurenet.com

Portfolio submissions
Send us your 3D artwork and you could be published in the magazine
portfolio@3dworldmag.com

Advertising
Ross Arthurs
Account sales manager
0207 042 4128
ross.arthurs@futurenet.com

Introducing our advisory board

Each issue, our panel of leading figures from across the CG industry give us their advice and help

Spotlight on...

Meet all of our advisory board members at **3dworldmag .com/board**

Jeremy Moorshead
**CHAIR, ANIMATION DEPARTMENT
SAVANNAH COLLEGE OF ART AND DESIGN**

Jeremy Moorshead began his career as animation cameraman at the National Film and Television School in the UK, and served as technical instructor at the Royal College of Art. He was a freelance animation cameraman for numerous independent shorts, including Nick Park's A Grand Day Out. Nominated for a Bafta for best animated short in 1997 for El Caminante, he currently heads the animation department at leading US college SCAD – which plays a prominent role in this issue's Get Ready for Animation, 3D World's bumper guide to 20 of the best animation and VFX schools in the world. See page 37 to secure your place!

Tim Alexander
VFX supervisor, ILM

Stuart Adcock
Technical art director,
Ninja Theory

Jordi Barés
3D creative director,
The Mill

Pascal Blanché
Art director,
Runescape, Jagex

Tim Brade
Technical director,
Aardman Animations

Rob Bredow
CTO, Sony Pictures
Imageworks

Gustavo Capote
Art director, Neoscape

Andrew Daffy
Director, The House
of Curves

Lee Danskin
Training development
director,
Escape Studios

Jonathan Davies
Executive producer,
Time Based Arts

Sofronis Efstathiou
MA 3D programme
leader, National Centre
for Computer Animation,
Bournemouth University

Paul Franklin
VFX supervisor,
Double Negative

Andrew Gordon
Directing animator, Pixar

Eddie Leon
President/CEO, Spine3D

Andrew Lindsay
Director of animation,
Lionhead Studios

Stefan Marjoram
Director, Aardman
Animations

Jeremy Moorshead
Animation department
chair, SCAD

Alex Morris
Founder,
Alex Morris Visualisation

Ximo Peris
Creative director,
Crystal CG

Shelley Page
Head of International
Outreach,
DreamWorks Animation

Robi Roncarelli
Editor and publisher,
PIXEL

Jolyon Webb
R&D art director,
Blitz Game Studios

This issue's contributors

Antony Ward
DIGITAL ARTIST

Antony has worked for some of today's top game studios, and has written numerous tutorials for magazines and websites. On page 72 he shows you how to rig tank tracks in Maya, while on page 78 he presents his top tips for character rigging.

Mike Griggs
CONCEPT DESIGNER

Mike is a concept designer working across 3D, motion graphics and VFX. In this issue he reveals projection mapping techniques in modo that can help to speed up your workflow (page 82) and explains how to model a human hand with ease (page 88).

Alex Telford
VFX ARTIST

Alex is a professional visual effects artist and certified Blender 3D instructor in New Zealand. He shares his expert knowledge of the software in his workshop on page 90, which looks at setting up phoneme libraries for more realistic facial animations.

Glen Southern
OWNER, SOUTHERNGFX

Glen is a freelance 3D artist with over 15 years' industry experience in film, TV and games. He's the owner of Cheshire-based SouthernGFX. Turn to page 96 for his tips on retopologising a mesh you've created in ZBrush for use in another program.

Tom Skelton
DIGITAL PRODUCER

Tom is a freelance digital producer based in Hertfordshire and his recent clients include Philips, Red&Pink and Sophie Hiller. Get creative with your projects as he walks you through the process of animating a shaped transition in After Effects on page 98.

EDITORIAL EDITOR Richard Hill richard.hill@futurenet.com **ART EDITOR** Darren Phillips darren.phillips@futurenet.com **DESIGNER** Shona Cutt shona.cutt@futurenet.com **PRODUCTION EDITOR** Sarah Edwardes sarah.edwardes@futurenet.com **TECHNICAL EDITOR** Rob Redman rob.redman@futurenet.com **STAFF WRITER** Kerrie Hughes kerrie.hughes@futurenet.com **ONLINE EDITOR** Kulsoom Middleton kulsoom.middleton@futurenet.com **NEW MEDIA EDITOR** Simon Arblaster simon.arblaster@futurenet.com **CONTRIBUTORS** Rose Brandle, Paul Champion, James Clarke, James Cutler, Mike Griggs, Andrew Gordon, Steve Jarratt, Christopher Kenworthy, David Pimentel, Mark Ramshaw, Steven Raynes, Mental Roy, Adam Sharp, Scott Spencer, Tom Skelton, Glen Southern, Fabio Stabel, Alex Telford, Antony Ward, Garrick Webster Cover Luis Arizaga Illustration Simon Cornish Image library iStockPhoto **SENIOR CREATIVES CREATIVE DIRECTOR** Robin Abbott **EDITORIAL DIRECTOR** Jim Douglas **ADVERTISING SENIOR SALES EXECUTIVE** Ross Arthurs +44 20 7042 4128 ross.arthurs@futurenet.com **SENIOR SALES EXECUTIVE** Laura Watson +44 20 7042 4122 laura.watson@futurenet.com **ACCOUNT SALES MANAGER** Ricardo Sidoli +44 20 7042 4124 ricardo.sidoli@futurenet.com **ADVERTISING SALES DIRECTOR** Nick Weatherall +44 20 7042 4155 nick.weatherall@futurenet.com **LONDON SALES DIRECTOR** Malcolm Stoodley +44 20 7042 4156 malcolm.stoodley@futurenet.com **PRINT & PRODUCTION PRODUCTION CONTROLLER** Marie Quilter marie.quilter@futurenet.com **PRODUCTION MANAGER** Mark Constance mark.constance@futurenet.com **LICENSING INTERNATIONAL LICENSING DIRECTOR** Tim Hudson tim.hudson@futurenet.com Telephone +44 1225 442244 Fax +44 1225 732275 **MARKETING MARKETING MANAGER – CREATIVE** Lyndsey Mayhew lyndsey.mayhew@futurenet.com **MARKETING EXECUTIVE** Sarah Jackson sarah.jackson@futurenet.com **CIRCULATION TRADE MARKETING MANAGER** Stuart Brown stuart.brown@futurenet.com **INTERNATIONAL ACCOUNT MANAGER** Richard Jefferies richard.jefferies@futurenet.com **TRADE MARKETING DIRECTOR** Rachael Cock rachael.cock@futurenet.com **FUTURE PUBLISHING LIMITED PUBLISHER & GROUP PUBLISHING DIRECTOR** Stuart Anderton stuart.anderton@futurenet.com **GROUP PUBLISHER** Matthew Pierce matthew.pierce@futurenet.com **CHIEF EXECUTIVE** Mark Wood **SUBSCRIPTIONS SUBSCRIBE ONLINE** myfavouritemagazines.co.uk **CALL OUR UK HOTLINE** 0844 848 2852 **US & CANADA: SUBSCRIBE AT** imsnews.com/3dworld **US HOTLINE** +1 800 428 3003. Printed in the UK by William Gibbons. Distributed in the UK by Seymour Distribution Ltd, 2 East Poultry Avenue, London EC1A 9PT. Tel +20 7429 4000

Next issue on sale 27 Mar 2012

Future produces carefully targeted magazines, websites and events for people with a passion. Our portfolio includes more than 180 magazines, websites and events and we export or license our publications to 90 countries around the world.

Future plc is a public company quoted on the London Stock Exchange (symbol: FUTR).

www.futureplc.com

CHIEF EXECUTIVE Mark Wood
NON-EXECUTIVE CHAIRMAN Peter Allen
GROUP FINANCE DIRECTOR Graham Harding
Tel +44 (0)20 7042 4000 (London)
+44 (0)1225 442244 (Bath)

Want to work for Future**?**
Visit www.futurenet.com/jobs

A member of the Audit Bureau of Circulations
12,842
Jan-Dec 2010

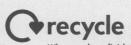
When you have finished with this magazine please recycle it.

QUADRO® FERMI
EXPONENTIALLY BETTER FOR 3DS MAX AND IRAY

NVIDIA PNY™

JOIN THE RENDERING REVOLUTION AND MAXIMIZE YOUR SPEED TO PHOTOREALISM WITH IRAY AND NVIDIA FERMI CLASS GPUs.

Take full advantage of Autodesk 3ds Max 2011 and realize photorealistic images with the new iray® ray-tracing capabilities. NVIDIA® Quadro® professional graphics solutions let you dial up the complexity of your designs, visualize them with photorealistic detail, and deliver higher quality results in less time.

Produce Higher Quality Images in Less Time
> 6x faster results over a quad-core CPU[2] when using an NVIDIA Quadro 5000 or NVIDIA Tesla™ C2050.

Interact Faster with your Design
> Featuring the new Scalable Geometry Engine and up to 6GB graphics memory, Fermi-based Quadro and Tesla GPUs provide maximum interactivity.

Scale iray Rendering Performance
> Use up to three Quadro or Tesla GPUs in your workstation to scale iray rendering speeds and to produce results faster than ever before.

RECOMMENDED QUADRO SOLUTIONS

MAX ARTIST

from £629

Quadro 4000
> 2 GB of frame buffer for texture heavy scenes
> 256 CUDA Cores
> 256-bit Memory Interface
> Up to 33% greater interactive performance**
> 3.5x speed up* for iray rendering

IRAY SPECIALIST

from £1472

Quadro 5000
> 2.5 GB of frame buffer for even heavier textured scenes
> 352 CUDA Cores
> 320-bit Memory Interface
> 5x speed up* for iray rendering

IRAY EXPERT

from £3081

Quadro 6000
> 6 GB of frame buffer for maximum textures
> 448 CUDA Cores
> 384-bit Memory Interface
> Up to + 50% greater interactive performance**
> Geometry Engines help large mesh models

To find out more go to **www.nvidia.co.uk/3dsmax** or one of our specialist solution providers below:

Insight
http://uk.insight.com/
Tel: 0844-846-3333

JIGSAW
Jigsaw
www.jigsaw24.com
Tel: 03332-400-888

SCAN
Scan Computers
www.scan.co.uk
Tel: 0871-472-4747

dabs.com
Dabs
http://www.dabs.com/quadro
Tel: 0870-429-3825

3D WORLD

Contents

Issue 154 *April 2012*

016

037

SUBSCRIBE AND
SAVE MONEY!
Get 3D World
delivered direct
and save up to 30%!
See page 34

028
25 TIPS ON ANIMATION
Top techniques, insider
tricks and essential books

072

Turn to page 114 to grab
your packed free disc

+ 3D WORLD

Community
Images and opinion
from you, the 3D
World readers

Portfolio

This month's selection of new 3D art
includes photorealistic watches, sci-fi
habitats and an homage to Tesla

▶ **Artist** Florian Autret
Title Quai de l'Ile
Software 3ds Max, mental ray, Nuke

"The name of this watch is Quai de l'Ile and it's made by Vacheron Constantin, a
Swiss watchmaker since 1755. I modelled it in 3ds Max, rendered with mental ray
and composited in Nuke. When modelling the watch I realised how complex the
luxury mechanisms are, and it was really exciting to reproduce it in 3D. I learned
a lot about the lighting – I tried many different techniques and aimed to bring out
the beautiful shapes of this watch.

"I learned 3D for two years at a French 3D school and worked for a two-month
training period at Le Truc in Switzerland, which does digital effects and post-
production for advertising. I'm currently working on my portfolio and searching
for a full-time job."
lawl_@hotmail.fr
yourprofolio.com/florianautret

66 As I modelled the watch I realised how complex the luxury mechanisms are 99

▶ Artist **Peter Nowacki**
Title **The Race Day**
Software **Maya, 3ds Max, V-Ray,
Photoshop, After Effects**
"I work as a junior 3D artist at Ars
Thanea and created this image
in my free time. It's based on a
concept by Gary Tonge (**antifan
real.deviantart.com/gallery/#/
d272xo0**). First I used Maya, then
I exported the whole scene to
3ds Max and used V-Ray. Textures
were done in Photoshop and final
composition and post-work in
After Effects.

"I used Maya's nCloth for a
great and really fast simulation for
the canopies at the top. I also
spent time on geometry
deformation on the walls and
props rather than just using bump
maps. I used many variations of
VrayDirt, too, mixing maps with
textures already painted by hand.
This gave me a more used and
natural look.

"The thing I enjoyed most
about creating this image was
that day after day it started to
look better and better, with every
detail making it more realistic.
Every little thing can inspire me,
from music to my environment.
I try to analyse simple details
around me all the time and keep
them in mind while modelling."
peter@velendil.com
velendil.com

❝ Seeing how the idea develops from the initial sketch is like a process of self-discovery ❞

▶ **Artist** Toni Bratincevic
Title Tesla
Software 3ds Max, ZBrush, Photoshop, Fusion

"I was a scene assembler at Blur Studio for almost four years, and am now working at Blizzard Entertainment as an environment artist in the cinematic department. This image is dedicated to one of the greatest inventors of all time, Nikola Tesla. To create it, I used 3ds Max, ZBrush for modelling, Photoshop for texture painting and Fusion for compositing.

"I used a nice feature in V-Ray called Shademap to render depth of field (DOF) in camera in a reasonable amount of time. It does a prepass without any DOF and motion blur, bakes that into a pointcloud map and reuses that pointcloud in final rendering with DOF on. This cuts down render time by almost 50 per cent in some cases.

"I enjoyed tweaking the camera to get the correct DOF and doing the compositing work on this image. Modelling and texturing were also fun – but I've got so used to them that I do it automatically. What I really like about every image I create is seeing how the idea develops from the initial sketch; it looks like a process of self-discovery."
toni@interstation3d.com
interstation3d.com

❝ Nearly everything can serve as a stimulus for the creation of new work ❞

▶ Artist **Nekrasov Alexandr**
Title **Sad Horse**
Software **3ds Max, Mudbox, V-Ray, Photoshop**

"I've been working in 3D for more than 10 years and am a CG artist at a small studio. My daughter's soft toy served as a character for this image and it took about a week and a half to finish. I began by photographing the toy from different perspectives, then used these photos as a resource for modelling and texturing. I did the modelling in 3ds Max and Mudbox, where I also painted the textures. I rendered in V-Ray using VrayFur for the coat and mane, and created the particles with Pflow. The final assembling was done in Photoshop.

"I create works like this in my free time. In order not to let my creativity die away in the technical routine, I try to be involved in several projects, interchanging them. Usually I like to take an object that really exists or characters invented by someone (for example, from the cinema) and to plunge them into unusual situations or surroundings. Nearly everything can serve as a stimulus for the creation of new work: a shot in a film or a photo, memories from childhood, something that caught my eye at that moment and so on. Inspiration can appear from nearly nothing."

nekrasoff-3d@yandex.ru
nekrasoff-3d.cgsociety.org

▲ Artist Sébastien Hue
Title **Terminal 13**
Software **Vue, 3ds Max, Photoshop, After Effects**
"This picture took me probably an entire week, if
I count all the hours I spent on modelling and
painting. I used a procedural terrain in Vue to
combine several cubic forms to generate the city.
It's unusual to model such a city in Vue, but I really
liked the approach. Once you understand the Terrain
editor functions and how to combine nodes and
filters, it's really powerful.

"I enjoyed creating the illusion of massive depth.
Imagine such a city, floating into space like this, so
huge that you can't even see where it ends. That's
the impact I wanted for the scene."
seb13digits@gmail.com
shue13-digital.13-digits.com

▶ Artist Cornelius Dämmrich
Title **Mercury**
Software **Cinema 4D, V-Ray, Photoshop, ZBrush**
"I study media design in Cologne, Germany, and do
occasional freelance jobs. It took me five weeks to
create this image and I enjoyed pushing myself to
generate more and more detail. The textures are my
own, but parts of the HDDs in front of the light tubes
are from TurboSquid, while the laptop near the pizza
box was made by Macray (**C4dnetwork.com**).

"I created the sheet with Cinema 4D Clothilde,
added some folds with ZBrush and put SSS and a
simple noise displacement map on it. It's a bit unusual
and kind of bungled… but it works. It looks a little like
foam – that wasn't planned, but I like it very much."
eimer@evoleeq.com
evoleeq.com

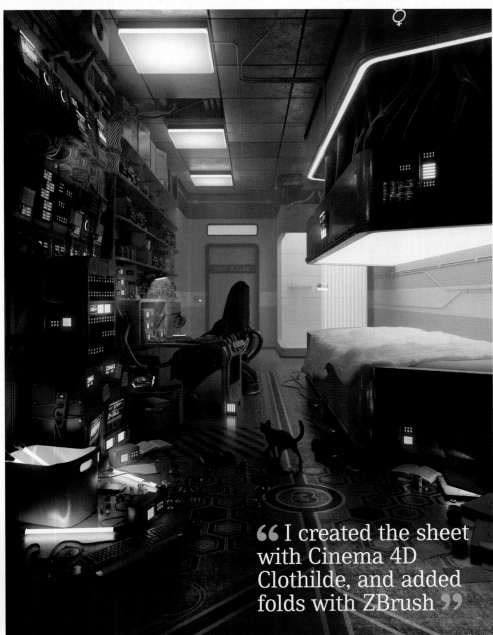

> **I created the sheet
with Cinema 4D
Clothilde, and added
folds with ZBrush**

Get published
If you would like to see
your work featured in
3D World, email us at the
address below, attaching a low-res
version of the image
portfolio@3dworldmag.com

Portfolio: *In focus*

Fabio Stabel of Blizzard Entertainment reveals how he painstakingly built his serene Chinese garden

◄ **Artist** Fabio Stabel
Title The Chinese Garden
Software 3ds Max, PlantStudio, Ivy Generator, Photoshop, mental ray, Fusion

"I first started using computer graphics back in 1995, and since then I've been trying to learn all aspects of it, from modelling to compositing and everything in between. I'm constantly trying to find ways to optimise my workflow in order to improve the quality of my final work. Currently, I'm a finisher at Blizzard Entertainment.

"The Chinese Garden is the only major personal project I've had in the past six years. I started it while beta testing 3ds Max 2012. I was inspired after reading an article in a magazine about Huntington Botanical Gardens in San Marino, California. I've used the time I've spent on it testing new ideas, implementing new techniques and learning more about the workflow in different areas."
fabiostabel.com

Stage 1
Creating the pavilion

▲ References collected from the web are useful for modelling, but not for shader development

01 Taking reference pictures
I could use references collected from the web for modelling purposes, but not as reference for shader development because the pictures were taken at different times of the day, from different angles and with various camera settings. Each image had different colours for the same structure. The relationship between lighting, cameras and shading are covered in more detail in step 5.

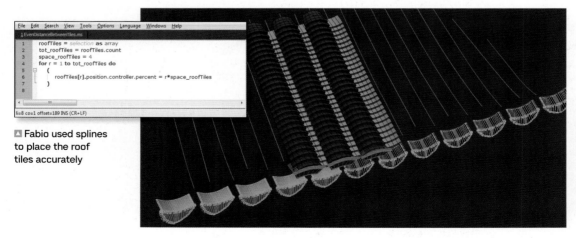

▲ Fabio used splines to place the roof tiles accurately

```
File  Edit  Search  View  Tools  Options  Language  Windows  Help
EvenDistanceBetweenTiles.ms
1   roofTiles = selection as array
2   tot_roofTiles = roofTiles.count
3   space_roofTiles = 4
4   for r = 1 to tot_roofTiles do
5     (
6       roofTiles[r].position.controller.percent = r*space_roofTiles
7     )
8
li=8 co=1 offset=189 INS (CR+LF)
```

02 Modelling the roof
I wanted the model to be as close as possible to the real pavilion. I counted the number of roof tiles on each row and modelled the same amount of tiles accordingly. Due to the curved shape of the roof and the high number of tiles per row, the best way to model the roof was using splines to preview the curvature, and as path controllers (without animation) to each tile. Using MaxScript, I could ensure that the tiles were evenly distributed across the spline. With the roof rigged, the modelling was a simple case of adjusting the curves' knots, then all the tiles would follow the splines. »

"The Chinese Garden is the only major personal project I've had in the past six years"

▲ Fabio took his own reference pictures so that he could create shaders that were true to life

03 Modelling the pavilion

The pavilion has the same external structure on each of its six sides, so after the completion of the first side, a clone rotation of 60 degrees helped to get the model completed. The pavilion's internal structure is asymmetrical but simple.

▲ The pavilion featured in the image has a hexagonal external structure

▲ The pavilion has six identical external faces, so clone rotation was used to model them quickly

04 Layout modelling and baseObject

For the modelling stage, I used a technique I like to call 'layout modelling'. I started creating low-resolution pieces and replaced them later on using MaxScript's baseObject property. This enabled me to get the final proportions and basic shapes without having to deal with heavy geometry on the viewport, when high-resolution details aren't needed. Each object in 3ds Max – meshes, lights and so on – has a property describing what sort of object it is. The baseObject property is the lowest item on the modifier stack and can easily be replaced.

This method can be used to create instanced objects out of a list of unique objects and even to replace different types of objects – for instance, meshes by lights. The only requirement for this to work is to have the pivot position in the same relative position in both low- and high-resolution objects: this way, when objects are replaced their relative position to the mesh is preserved.

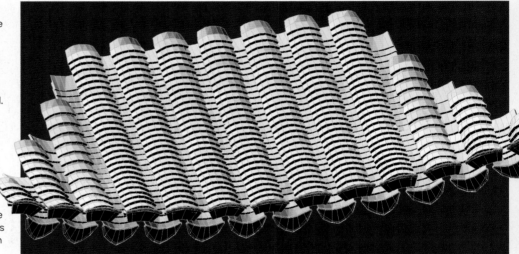

05 Camera response, light and shaders

One aspect I like to pay attention to when creating shaders is the relationship they have with the light source and the camera response. In order for shaders to respond correctly to camera and light, it's important to know that the light on the 3D scene has the same intensity as the light in the reference picture, and that the camera on the 3D scene has the same exposure values as the camera used to take the reference picture. Otherwise, the shader will be created based on

wrong information and will deviate from the target material.

I decided to visit the place and take some pictures myself. From those pictures I got all the necessary information, so I could lock down the correct camera response and light source. I then inputted the exposure value, the exact GPS location and the time taken from my photos to 3ds Max. The sun and sky intensities were created with mental ray's Daylight System. I could also get the correct pavilion alignment from Google Earth, recreating the same lighting condition (angle and intensity) and camera response from the reference pictures. At this point, if the shader looks the same in my test renders as the real material from the reference picture, I know that the shader is close to physically correct and will give the correct response under any lighting condition on the 3D scene.

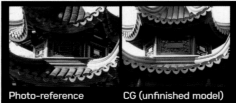

Photo-reference   CG (unfinished model)

Stage 2
The fine details

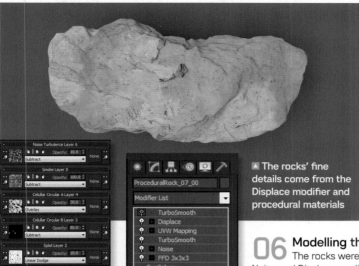

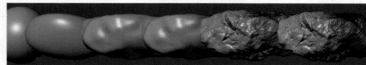

▲ The rocks' fine details come from the Displace modifier and procedural materials

06 Modelling the rocks

The rocks were modelled out of geodesic spheres with TurboSmooth, Noise and Displace modifiers. The Noise modifier gives the basic shape, changing the model before the subdivisions, and each rock has a different seed. Fine detail comes from the Displace modifier and a combination of procedural materials.

▲ Each of the rocks has a different seed so that it has a unique shape and size

07 Blades of grass

The grass in the scene is made out of single geometric blades that are grouped, collapsed together and then converted into mental ray proxies. The use of proxies helps memory management during rendering time, because the geometry doesn't need to be present in the memory all the time – it's loaded only when rays intersect their bounding boxes. This way, the geometry is not allocated in 3ds Max and is only loaded when actually needed. mental ray proxies don't need to be converted because they're already in mental ray binary format.

▶ Proxies are used to help memory management during rendering

09 Creating vegetation

For the small vegetation, I used GuruWare's Ivy Generator (guruware.at/main) and Plant Studio (kurtz-fernhout.com/PlantStudio). The plant library was converted to mental ray proxies.

▶ Plant models were converted to mental ray proxies

08 The water

Other than the regular key water components such as reflection, refraction and bump map, I included the Parti Volume shader on its volume component, which brings the murky look and creates underwater volumetric shadows. Submerged objects fade out realistically based on how deep they are. The water colour is defined by the Parti Volume colour but also receives some influence from the lake's bottom. For the water a box was used (instead of a plane) for the right volumetric representation.

10 Scripts

Other than some small MaxScripts, I developed two main scripts: Transforms and CreateBranches. The first script was for mental ray proxy management – I needed to be able to switch between mental ray proxies and geometry (it's impossible to see geometric intersections with point clouds), mass edit for point cloud densities and transformations, random selection and scattering of mental ray proxies. Since mental ray proxies can't be scattered or used as particles, this script was useful for the creation of multiple instances of grass patches and the connection to the ground surface. The second script was designed for modelling branches and trees, which is explained in more detail in step 11.

▶ Scripts were created to handle mental ray proxy management and for modelling trees

■ New branches are created from previous iterations

11 The trees

I tried to use royalty-free models from the web, but apart from the trees from **3dmentor.ru** (which were used on the background) I couldn't find high-res models with leaves properly connected to the branches for the foreground. I then decided to create a branch editor – a small system based on splines. The system is far from being a production-proven tool; I stopped its development as soon as I reached some basic functionality. The script creates random splines out of a selected spline. The closer the new branch is to the end of the parent branch, the smaller it will be. The process can be repeated over and over, selecting previously created branches and creating new ones. Newly created branches are path-connected to their parent branches, so the editing is somewhat easy – if the parent branch is edited, the child branches will remain connected. When the spline layout is done, the script creates the 3D branches and applies a basic UVW Unwrap operation based on the spline used for its shape. The leaf creation has the same approach. Selected branches receive randomly created leaves. Probably 80 per cent of the visible trees were modelled using this script.

▲ Fabio wrote his own branch editor script, which creates random splines

Stage 3
Finishing touches

12 Dividing up the scene

The scene was divided into areas (the far background, background trees, the island, the pavilion and so on), with each area being a single isolated scene. The main scene cross-referenced all the pieces together. The render time was about 24 hours for the Final Gathering generation plus 48 hours for the final render, at 3,000x4,000 pixels with 4 and 16 anti-alias samples.

13 Compositing

The project was designed to be rendered in one single pass and mental ray proxies helped a lot with this, but with the image almost finished I decided to add more details – basically displacements and small fixes. Other than some colour corrections, small changes and render elements balance, the compositing phase was important to add these fixes. This was a long and fun project, and I had the opportunity to learn a lot from it. I'm looking forward to the next one! ●

01

SQUASH AND STRETCH

Your animated objects should compress and stretch as they move. As a simple example, think of a rubber ball that flattens slightly as it hits the ground; but the principle applies equally to muscles in the body, for example. Squash and stretch is most obvious in exaggerated or cartoony animation, but applies to realistic styles too. In realistic animation, the volume of the object should remain constant as it stretches.

◢ Drown to Life shows great use of squash and stretch in its faces

02

ANTICIPATION

Prepare the audience for a major movement or change. As a simple example, think of a golf swing where you would show the club going backwards first. But you could equally show a character's head turning towards a door before someone enters the room, or an object becoming the focal point in the camera frame before someone picks it up.

◢ You know just what's going to happen in this frame from Will & the Wheel

»

03

STAGING

Present only essential information to enable the audience to understand what's happening. The concept of staging employs everything from the character action to the environment, colour palette and camera placement to represent the idea you want to communicate. Each sequence in your animation should depict the most important idea at that stage.

▶ This scene from Defective Detective is beautifully staged

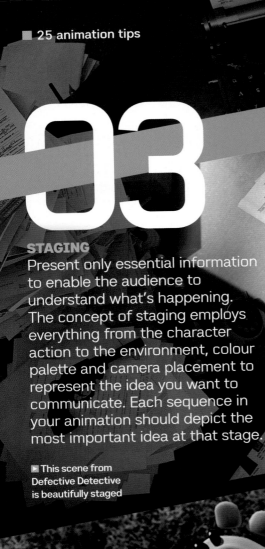

◀ The Avery-inspired moves in Elk Hair Caddis rely on overlapping action

04

STRAIGHT-AHEAD ACTION AND POSE-TO-POSE

Two different approaches to drawing animation poses. Straight-ahead action means drawing each frame in your sequence consecutively, while pose-to-pose means drawing the key poses first, and then filling in the intermediate frames. The latter approach will intuitively feel more natural to most computer animators, who are used to keyframe-based tools, but straight-ahead action traditionally leads to more fluid movement: bear its benefits in mind as you animate.

05

FOLLOW-THROUGH AND OVERLAPPING ACTION

Two methods of making your characters feel more lifelike. Follow-through means that some parts of a body or object will continue moving even after a major action has ended; think of a plate of jelly as you place it on a table, for example. Overlapping action describes the tendency for different parts of a body or object to complete a main action at different speeds.

5 ANIMATOR TIPS FROM ANDREW GORDON

1 THINK AHEAD
Planning for a shot is just as important as animating. It lets you think about where you're going before you jump in and start moving things. Make it a ritual.

2 MAKE YOUR CHARACTERS STILL
Many animators feel the need to move the character around a lot. Take cues from film actors: try to hold poses and act within a pose.

3 FIND FRESH MOVEMENTS
When using gestures to animate, be careful not to use cliché gestures. Clichés are those gestures that you see a lot. Think of new and interesting ways of doing a gesture. Pull from around you by looking at friends, relatives, co-workers and different age groups.

4 CONCEIVE SPLINES AS A GROUP
When editing splines, it's good practice to group splines together that relate to one another. For example, if you were polishing the torso of a character, you'd want to see the root, spine, neck and head. They all work together, so it's important to polish them together.

5 DON'T CUT CORNERS WITH DIALOGUE
If you're animating a dialogue shot and don't have much time to polish, at the very least, pay attention to how much the jaw moves, and the corners moving in and out and up and down.

06

SLOW IN AND SLOW OUT

Start and end a sequence with slower movement. Few natural movements reach their peak speed immediately, so devote more frames to the start and end of an action than to the high-speed middle part of the action.

► Meet Meline's graceful movement is derived from slow-in, slow-out

07

ARCS

Follow a natural arc in the movement of a character or object. Few objects in nature move in a straight line; instead, create an arc for the extreme point of the object to follow. Keep physical laws in mind: a fast-moving object will typically require a wider arc than a slow object while turning a corner, for example.

◄ Fins, plants, water... Hooked abounds with secondary action

3 MUST-HAVE **ANIMATION TOOLS** FOR MAYA

1 ANDY RIG
Free from studentpages. scad.edu/~jdoubl20/ rigsScripts.html
Created by John Doublestein with help from Craig Scheuermann and Ying-Chih Chen, Andy (short for 'androgynous') is a generic character rig suitable for both male and female characters. It was created for students at Savannah College of Art and Design, but is available to all animation students for use or study.

2 RAPID RIG ADVANCED
$20 from rapidrig.com
Created by BioWare artist Dustin Nelson, Rapid Rig Advanced offers a script-driven user interface aiming to make it easier and quicker to rig a newly modelled biped character. You make your custom choices, then Rapid Rig creates the controls, with locking for knees and elbows; orientation controls for hips, eyes, head and shoulders; and more.

3 VOICE-O-MATIC
$349 from di-o-matic.com
This plug-in for Maya (separate versions for 3ds Max and Softimage are also available) speeds up the process of animating dialogue by automatically matching movement to imported audio. Whether you're using blend shapes or full-blown rigs, Voice-o-Matic produces accurate keyframes that you can readily tweak to suit your needs.

08

SECONDARY ACTION

Use small supporting actions to emphasise your main action. Breathe life into your character by adding secondary actions, but don't allow them to distract from your central idea for the sequence. A character walking may swing its arms jauntily or place its hands in its pockets according to the overall mood you wish to establish, for instance.

INSIDER TIP
"Make good choices in your storytelling. Allow your characters to really believe their story and react to it in a way only they would. Let your audience see their choices on screen and the effects of those choices"
Dave Pimentel, head of story, DreamWorks

3 MUST-HAVE ANIMATION BOOKS FOR YOUR SHELF

1 DRAWN TO LIFE

Walt Stanchfield

VOL 1 tinyurl.com/drawntolife1
VOL 2 tinyurl.com/drawntolife2

For over 20 years, Disney animator Walt Stanchfield gave classes inside Walt Disney Animation Studios, providing insight and inspiration to artists including Brad Bird. The two volumes of Drawn to Life compile his notes and sketches by both himself and his students, providing the best possible primer for anyone learning the art and craft of animation.

SAMPLE TIP

"A sure way to keep from making static, lifeless drawing is to think of drawing verbs instead of nouns... Let's say, for example, the model is leaning over with her elbows extended. If you approach the pose from the standpoint of drawing nouns, you will name and draw the parts (biceps, triceps, etc) and place them as best you can in the positions suggested by the model.

"If you approach the pose from the standpoint of drawing verbs, you will simply be using those nouns to produce a drawing that portrays a woman, bending over, stretching her arms, pulling her hair... You feel she is thinking about what she is doing – not just frozen into a still life."

2 THE ANIMATOR'S SURVIVAL KIT

Richard Williams

tinyurl.com/animatorkit

Richard Williams has more than 40 years' experience in the industry, across both hand-drawn and computer animation. Based on his acclaimed Animation Masterclasses, The Animator's Survival Kit sets out the key principles of animation.

SAMPLE TIP

"The major beginner's mistake is doing too much action in too short a space of time. The remedy: go twice as slow...

"Ken Harris told me that when Ben Washam was starting out at Warner's, he became famous for 'Benny's 12-Frame Yawn'. Ben drew well and made 12 elaborate drawings of someone going through the broad motions of a yawn. Then he shot it on ones. Zip! It flashed through in half a second! So then he shot it on twos. ZZZip! It went through in one second! So then he inbetweened (24 drawings now) and shot it on twos. ZZZZZZ! It went through in two seconds – almost right.

"Then Ken showed him how to add some cushioning drawings at the beginning and end – and bingo, Ben's on his way to being a fine animator."

3 TIMING FOR ANIMATION

Harold Whitaker & John Halas

tinyurl.com/timinganimation

John Halas co-directed and co-produced 1954's Animal Farm, the UK's first animated feature film, for which Harold Whitaker was a key member of the animation department. The two collaborated on Timing for Animation, which delves into the relationship between the drawing and the frame like never before. Topics covered include how to use timing to suggest speed or the lack of it. The second edition updates the core material with segments by Tom Sito to address digital production.

SAMPLE TIP

"There is a train of cause and effect which runs through an object when it is acted upon by a force. This is the result of the transmission of the force through a more or less flexible medium (ie, caricatured matter). This is one aspect of good movement in animation.

"An animator must understand the mechanics of the natural movement of an object and then keep this knowledge in the back of their mind whilst concentrating on the real business of animation. This is the creation of mood and conveying the right feeling by the way an action is done."

09

TIMING

Use the appropriate number of frames for a given action. Consider how long an action should take in nature and restrict the number of frames you use accordingly.

10

EXAGGERATION

Exaggerate elements in your sequence to inject life into it. Animation that strives to imitate real life with precision often appears lifeless instead. Deploy exaggeration in the form of movement, physical proportions or style to bring your animation to life. Even realistic animation can benefit from carefully considered exaggeration.

◄ Defective Detective
shows the impact of
solid-feeling forms

11

SOLID DRAWING

Conceive objects in three dimensions, with volume and depth. Classical principles of drawing encourage the artist to capture the form of an object rather than just its shape, so that the onlooker has a sense of the unseen areas of an object and how they affect other objects or the light within a scene, for example. Even in 3D animation, take care not to allow your objects to look flat.

12

APPEAL

Develop traits in your character that encourage the audience to sympathise with it. The principle of appeal doesn't simply mean that the audience should like all of your characters, more that they can project themselves into the character and understand how they're feeling. Even villains should have appeal. ●

◼ Appeal matters
even in realistic
animation like Sintel

THANKS TO...

ANDREW GORDON
Best-known for his animation contributions to Pixar greats including Toy Story 2 and 3, The Incredibles, Ratatouille, and Finding Nemo, Andrew is also part of the Animation Collaborative, a regular series of workshops offering small-class training with working professionals.
animationcollaborative.com

ADAM SHARP
Adam is a freelance CG artist and film-maker. His work includes ads, music videos, TV series and short films, including The Curse of the Last Child.
adamations.co.uk

DAVID PIMENTEL
David has worked in animation for over 17 years and currently works as head of story for DreamWorks. His recent credits include Bee Movie, How to Train Your Dragon and the short Kung Fu Panda: Secrets of the Masters. He's also written Evoke, a compilation of sketches and drawing and animation lessons.
drawingsfromamexican.
blogspot.com

9 TIPS FROM SCAD'S **SCOTT WRIGHT** IN **GET READY FOR ANIMATION** SEE PAGE 60

US AND CANADA
Fantastic subs offer **SAVE $82**

3D WORLD

V-Ray + Blender + Maya + ZBrush

WORLD **#1** FOR 3D ARTISTS

DO YOU REALLY NEED PHOTOSHOP?
3D-friendly alternatives to Adobe's image editor

32 PAGES OF 3D TUTORIALS
Toon sculpting • Renders in Blender • Maya particles

RENDER PASSES MADE EASY
Improve your output with simple steps

THE ART OF LIGHT
Bring pro photographer techniques into your CG

FREE MODEL
On this issue's disc: Victoria 5, as sold for $39
See page 112

Landscapes in 3ds Max
Expert ways to enhance

Great reasons to subscribe

- **Save up to 30%*** on a subscription
- **FREE** disc in every issue with assets and training
- Have 3D World delivered direct to your door every month, and never miss an issue again
- Stay up to date with 3D World's expert analysis and opinions, and see inspiring artwork

Maya + ZBrush + After Effects + modo +

3D WORLD

WORLD **#1** FOR 3D ARTISTS

CG CC GUIDE
Find animatio

FREE DISC
60 mins of V-Ray videos plus a texture bonanza
See page 114

RIGGII FOR GAME
20 ways to bring y characters to

GET AHEAD IN ANIMATION
Expert tips from great 3D animators & the best animation schools

SET UP TANK TRACKS IN MAYA
Script a versatile rig for vehicles and robots

PROJECTION MAPS
DYNAMESH TIPS
DEPTH OF FIELD

TECHNIQUE
MODEL A
Anatomy tips all fingers and

SUBSCRIBE TO 3D WORLD TODAY!

IAPES
emes to rs talking

US/Canada Subscriber?
Save over $82
Pay $31.25 every 3 months by continuous credit card
OR $124.99 for 13 issues
Subscribe online at www.imsnews.com/3dworld-a022
Call toll-free on **1-800-428-3003** and quote code: a022

TERMS AND CONDITIONS
*Savings compared to buying 13 issues from newsstand. **Savings compared to buying 13 issues at $15.99 at US newsstand. ROW and Europe have no set newsstand price, and therefore we can't advertise the specific savings you will make. UK, EU, ROW will be charged in GBP. USA & Canada will be charged in USD. Minimum subscription term is 12 months. You will receive 13 issues of 3D World a year. If you are dissatisfied in any way during the next 60 days, please notify us in writing and we will refund all unmailed items. Full details of the direct debit guarantee will be provided and are available upon request. Your subscription will start with the next available issue. **Offer ends 31 May 2012.**

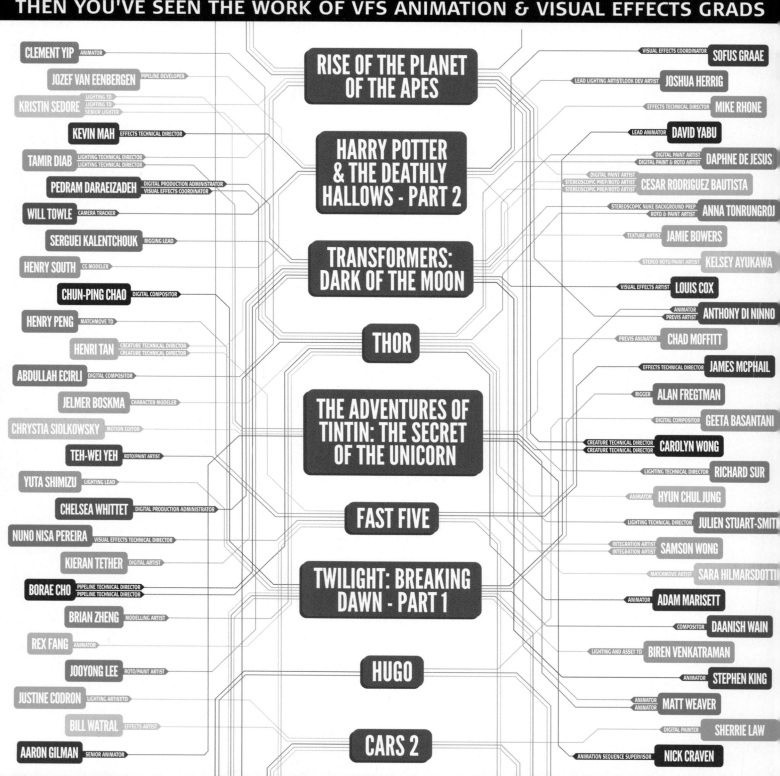

WATCHED A BLOCKBUSTER LATELY?

THEN YOU'VE SEEN THE WORK OF VFS ANIMATION & VISUAL EFFECTS GRADS

CLEMENT YIP — ANIMATOR

JOZEF VAN EENBERGEN — PIPELINE DEVELOPER

KRISTIN SEDORE — LIGHTING TD / LIGHTING TD / SENIOR LIGHTER

KEVIN MAH — EFFECTS TECHNICAL DIRECTOR

TAMIR DIAB — LIGHTING TECHNICAL DIRECTOR / LIGHTING TECHNICAL DIRECTOR

PEDRAM DARAEIZADEH — DIGITAL PRODUCTION ADMINISTRATOR / VISUAL EFFECTS COORDINATOR

WILL TOWLE — CAMERA TRACKER

SERGUEI KALENTCHOUK — RIGGING LEAD

HENRY SOUTH — CG MODELER

CHUN-PING CHAO — DIGITAL COMPOSITOR

HENRY PENG — MATCHMOVE TD

HENRI TAN — CREATURE TECHNICAL DIRECTOR / CREATURE TECHNICAL DIRECTOR

ABDULLAH ECIRLI — DIGITAL COMPOSITOR

JELMER BOSKMA — CHARACTER MODELER

CHRYSTIA SIOLKOWSKY — MOTION EDITOR

TEH-WEI YEH — ROTO/PAINT ARTIST

YUTA SHIMIZU — LIGHTING LEAD

CHELSEA WHITTET — DIGITAL PRODUCTION ADMINISTRATOR

NUNO NISA PEREIRA — VISUAL EFFECTS TECHNICAL DIRECTOR

KIERAN TETHER — DIGITAL ARTIST

BORAE CHO — PIPELINE TECHNICAL DIRECTOR / PIPELINE TECHNICAL DIRECTOR

BRIAN ZHENG — MODELLING ARTIST

REX FANG — ANIMATOR

JOOYONG LEE — ROTO/PAINT ARTIST

JUSTINE CODRON — LIGHTING ARTIST/TD

BILL WATRAL — EFFECTS ARTIST

AARON GILMAN — SENIOR ANIMATOR

Films
- RISE OF THE PLANET OF THE APES
- HARRY POTTER & THE DEATHLY HALLOWS - PART 2
- TRANSFORMERS: DARK OF THE MOON
- THOR
- THE ADVENTURES OF TINTIN: THE SECRET OF THE UNICORN
- FAST FIVE
- TWILIGHT: BREAKING DAWN - PART 1
- HUGO
- CARS 2

VISUAL EFFECTS COORDINATOR — SOFUS GRAAE

LEAD LIGHTING ARTIST/LOOK DEV ARTIST — JOSHUA HERRIG

EFFECTS TECHNICAL DIRECTOR — MIKE RHONE

LEAD ANIMATOR — DAVID YABU

DIGITAL PAINT ARTIST / DIGITAL PAINT & ROTO ARTIST — DAPHNE DE JESUS

DIGITAL PAINT ARTIST / STEREOSCOPIC PREP/ROTO ARTIST / STEREOSCOPIC PREP/ROTO ARTIST — CESAR RODRIGUEZ BAUTISTA

STEREOSCOPIC NUKE BACKGROUND PREP / ROTO & PAINT ARTIST — ANNA TONRUNGROJ

TEXTURE ARTIST — JAMIE BOWERS

STEREO ROTO/PAINT ARTIST — KELSEY AYUKAWA

VISUAL EFFECTS ARTIST — LOUIS COX

ANIMATOR / PREVIS ARTIST — ANTHONY DI NINNO

PREVIS ANIMATOR — CHAD MOFFITT

EFFECTS TECHNICAL DIRECTOR — JAMES MCPHAIL

RIGGER — ALAN FREGTMAN

DIGITAL COMPOSITOR — GEETA BASANTANI

CREATURE TECHNICAL DIRECTOR / CREATURE TECHNICAL DIRECTOR — CAROLYN WONG

LIGHTING TECHNICAL DIRECTOR — RICHARD SUR

ANIMATOR — HYUN CHUL JUNG

LIGHTING TECHNICAL DIRECTOR — JULIEN STUART-SMITH

INTEGRATION ARTIST / INTEGRATION ARTIST — SAMSON WONG

MATCHMOVE ARTIST — SARA HILMARSDOTTIR

ANIMATOR — ADAM MARISETT

COMPOSITOR — DAANISH WAIN

LIGHTING AND ASSET TD — BIREN VENKATRAMAN

ANIMATOR — STEPHEN KING

ANIMATOR / ANIMATOR — MATT WEAVER

DIGITAL PAINTER — SHERRIE LAW

ANIMATION SEQUENCE SUPERVISOR — NICK CRAVEN

VFS CONNECTS THE ENTERTAINMENT INDUSTRY.

VFS ANIMATION & VISUAL EFFECTS

LEARN MORE AT VFS.COM/3DWORLD

COMPUTER GRAPHICS STUDENT AWARDS
SCHOOL OF THE YEAR 2010 & 2011
cgCOACH

Welcome

20 of the best animation schools, and how to get in

Animation schools are the best way to develop your craft so that you can create your best work. Whether you're looking to animate the next Oscar-winning short or start a career with a studio, only schools offer the immersive and intensive experience that gives you the best possible foundation.

This selection of animation and visual effects schools is designed to give you a flavour of what's available. You'll discover how courses work, what they offer and what life as a student is like. But with stiff competition, you may have to fight for your place at a top-flight location. So we've asked schools what they're looking for in their applicants. Take their advice and you could find yourself at the head of the queue.

We've also asked SCAD animation professor Scott Wright, who was with DreamWorks Animation for 15 years, to offer his tips for all animators, whether you're a seasoned pro or are just setting out on your journey.

We expect...

Competition to get into the best animation and VFX schools is tough, so we've asked our spotlighted faculties what they expect from their best applicants. Take their advice on board when you apply and you could find yourself at the head of the entrance queue!

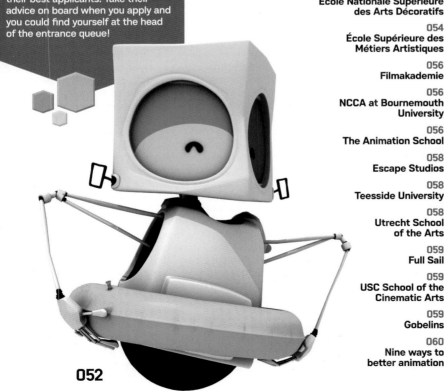

052

042

046

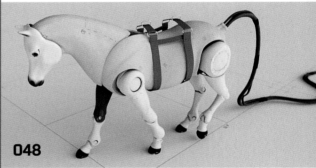

048

050

053

How to find your ideal animation school

Your journey towards your new animation or VFX career starts here. Find out how to choose the school that will give you the grounding you need

▲ Student work from Ringling College of Art and Design, Florida

Although you can get started with CG animation and visual effects and develop your skills with the help of training DVD, online courses, books and magazine tutorials, there's nothing quite like the experience you get from going back to school. Animation schools immerse you in the art and craft of CG, giving you access to film-making facilities and software pipelines based on those of professional studios. They use teaching staff drawn from the industry, plus guest lecturers who remain active today. And perhaps most importantly, they enable you to live the life of an animator for as long as you're on the course, sharing your experiences with other students learning in the same way.

None of this is a substitute for you doing the hard work, of course, but the best animation schools make sure their students are equipped for a CG industry hungry for new talent. "We make students employable," says Marty Hasselbach, managing director of Vancouver Film School. "Since the school replicates a studio environment, graduates hit the ground running. We also stack the deck in their favour by making sure they have an effective reel, and by bringing in many talent-hungry industry representatives to assess student work."

> "When you go to art school, you have to love what you're doing, and be willing to work day and night. That passion has to be there"
> Peter Weishar, dean, SCAD

What to look for

There are hundreds of animation courses to choose between, and even the local college down the road – never mind a top-flight academy in another city or country – represents a significant financial commitment. So being sure you have chosen the right faculty has never been more important.

Think carefully about whether you need a general grounding in 3D alongside other disciplines, in case a broad multimedia course is just the ticket; or whether only the deepest CG-only experience will satisfy your thirst for learning. Either way, you've immediately ruled out a large number of possibilities.

Next, form a shortlist and research each school. (Our guides in this issue should make this job a lot quicker, of course.) Ask each school about its connections with the industry. Find out what experience the staff have in the industry, and how recent that experience is – if you view the school as a route to employment, you need to be learning the latest practices.

Use YouTube and Vimeo to check out showreels and shorts produced by both current students and graduates at your target schools. Obviously you want to assess their technical quality – but more crucially, use the shorts to get a flavour of the type and variety of work a school's students are producing, and ask yourself which school is making the work that you want to create as well.

Although your school of choice should be well equipped, the intangible qualities and culture of a school matter more than whether they offer Cintiq touchscreens to work from. "If you focus on what you love, rather than follow industry trends, you'll find the right program," says Marianne Reilly, who heads

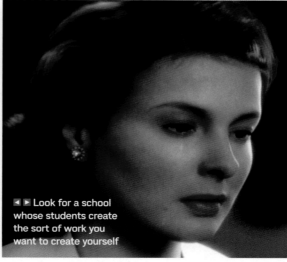

◀ ▶ Look for a school whose students create the sort of work you want to create yourself

Vancouver Film School's one-year 3D Animation and Visual Effects course. "It's all about where your passion lies!"

Passion is also the key word for Peter Weishar, dean of SCAD's School of Film, Digital Media and Performing Arts. "When you go to art school, you really have to love what you'll be doing, and be willing to work on it day and night," he says. "That passion has to be there."

Landing a job

Most people applying for animation school view it as bridge to employment in the CG industry, so you also need to find out what your target schools do to help you get that first job. If a school doesn't publish its graduate employment rates, ask for them. If they can't provide those figures, ask them why not.

More intangibly, try to get a sense of how well each school might prepare you for work. For Peter Weishar, it means equipping students with the right attitude and approach to their craft, which goes beyond knowing which keyboard shortcut to use. "Different studios do ask for different things, but usually what they're really after is a great aesthetic and an understanding of animation. VFX is a little different, in that the reel needs to demonstrate problem solving, whereas when it comes to animation it's really all about story and character. However, I think the days are gone when they would hire somebody based on raw talent, and then teach them how to use the computer later."

If you want to get into the best animation schools, you need to be ready to give as much as you receive – and for the best students, that hard work starts before they complete the application form. Marty Hasselbach stresses how important it is to do your homework. "Ask questions; talk to students, graduates and industry," he advises. "No two schools are alike, and a student needs to find the one that best suits their learning style and career objectives." ●

▲ Well-equipped facilities are clearly important, but creativity matters just as much

Savannah College of Art and Design

scad.edu

The School of Film, Digital Media and Performing Arts at SCAD offers a breadth and depth of teaching that attracts high-flying students from across the globe

Savannah is one of the oldest and most culturally rich cities in the United States. It has a long-standing reputation as a genteel, slow-paced Southern outpost; but in truth, it's always been a hive of activity, first as an agricultural hub, and then as home to one of the country's busiest ports. A key educational hotspot, the Savannah College of Art and Design was co-founded in 1978 by current president Paula Wallace.

SCAD's diverse student body, consisting of more than 11,000 students, comes from all 50 United States and more than 100 countries worldwide. The university offers degrees in more than 40 areas of study, as well as minors in nearly 60 disciplines in Savannah and Atlanta, Georgia; in Hong Kong; in Lacoste, France; and online through SCAD eLearning.

> ## "An undergraduate accepted into SCAD has a full year of foundation courses, and to help them decide on a path we hold a major fair"
> Peter Weishar, dean, SCAD

Peter Weishar is dean for SCAD's School of Film and Digital Media and Performing Arts. A veteran commercial artist, author and Siggraph presenter, he first moved into teaching at NYU, before joining SCAD eight years ago. He cites the college's breadth of teaching as one of the big attractions. "I loved teaching at NYU. It's a magnificent school, but the kind of range here is something I've never seen anywhere else. Yes, we're big, but it means that people can come here and study what they love with real depth. If you're going to be at one place for four years, you have to ask, do you want to shop at a boutique, or have the run of an entire department store?"

The School of Film, Digital Media and Performing Arts currently has some 2,700 students studying across 11 different programmes at both undergraduate and graduate level – the most popular of which is animation, with 857 currently enrolled. A further 278 are studying visual effects, 224 are studying motion media, and 449 are studying interactive design and

game development. "Our main digital media building in Savannah has about 600 CPUs," says Weishar, "and then we have a digital media centre in Atlanta, with beautiful new studios including greenscreen and motion-capture stages, plus a couple of hundred CPUs. Atlanta is a hub of cable television in the States, so there are a lot of opportunities for students there to intern and work out in the field. It's the smaller campus, however. In contrast, Savannah is a small town with a big school."

In 2010, SCAD also opened the doors to a campus in Hong Kong. Ostensibly, it was intended to provide local students with a centre of excellence for digital media studies, but Weishar says that those studying Stateside can also benefit. "Our students here can study in Hong Kong for 10 weeks or even an entire academic year. They can experience a different city and vibrant culture while following the same curriculum and never leaving the university."

Finding a career path

Students enrolling for graduate programmes are likely to have some idea of their desired career path, but things aren't so cut-and-dried when it comes to undergraduates, particularly those considering animation and visual effects. "A lot of students have the raw talent, but aren't yet sure what route to take," says Weishar. "An undergraduate accepted into SCAD has a full year of foundation courses, and then to help decide on a path we hold a major fair. We have lectures and presentations, and each major department sets up their own booth to talk to students and show examples of work. We give them the time and the information to think carefully about what they want to do."

While it isn't a trade school by any means, Weishar says that SCAD puts a very strong emphasis on career. "There's recognition that in order to express yourself artistically, you'll need a certain level of craft ability," he explains. "What we try to do is to promote the right combination of studio *and* aesthetic skills."

Equipping students with the practical production skills required by the industry while satisfying the broad goals of a liberal arts education is recognised as one of the key conundrums within accredited education. It's something Weishar says they address on a daily basis: "It would be arrogant of me to say we have the answer, and we're always

Location: Savannah, USA
Tel: +1 800 869 7223

► A still from RoboCareer, created by VFS student Steve Middleton

We expect...

Passion, maturity, an open mind and a hard-working attitude. VFS is also looking for people with an eye for detail and composition, and ideally some digital texture painting skills in Photoshop. You'll need to be a team player who is ready to work with people from all over the world

► The film school also runs a Classical Animation programme

◄ VFS students are taught how to engage their audiences

employment. For O'Reilly, fostering links with the industry is a key part of her role, and having the industry on the doorstep means a good range of quality instructors are available.

"My focus is on creating a bridge between the industry and students, which is effective in a hot West Coast market," says O'Reilly. "Vancouver is a great place for a graduate to find a job. Our instructors bring more of that industry experience as well; in fact, many of us worked together years ago on features as the market was expanding. Several are former supervisors in their fields, and we're lucky to have them as instructors."

Vancouver is a great place to be, as anyone who went to Siggraph last year will attest. There are the trendy bars down in Yaletown and on Commercial Drive, top-quality skiing is just an hour away, and nearby Stanley Park offers a peaceful break in the middle of the city. "Although VFS students spend the vast majority of their time working on their creative projects – after all, that's why they're here – Vancouver offers plenty of opportunities to relax and inspire them. The city's multicultural atmosphere means there's always something happening in the restaurant, arts and cultural scenes," concludes O'Reilly. ●

► Angelo De Witt's VFS reel helped him secure a position at The Mill

ESCAC: Film and Audiovisual School of Catalonia

escac.es

Barcelona's multi-award winning ESCAC film school has created an astonishing number of artists now at the forefront of the Spanish film industry

Europe has a rich tradition of animation and visual effects, and now, more than ever, the distinctions between these disciplines are converging. So, if you like the idea of following in the footsteps of graduates who have gone on to key creative roles on feature films such as Hellboy 2: The Golden Army and Pan's Labyrinth, then ESCAC could offer you the education and training you're looking for.

The Film and Audiovisual School of Catalonia (ESCAC) is a state-of-the-art institution that primes its students for the film industry. ESCAC has more than 20 years' experience in delivering high-quality training in filmmaking. Students study in a 6,000m^2 building in Terrassa and at a training and VFX centre based in Barcelona, a city that's quickly becoming a post-production hub.

ESCAC provides intensive training in the latest VFX techniques so that when students complete their courses, they can use their expertise to work in both national and international studios. "All of our teachers are working professionals," ESCAC marketing director Aritz Lekuona explains, "and in their own words, they don't teach students – rather, they train their future colleagues."

The school is ranked as one of the best film and audiovisual schools in the world, according to the leading magazines in the sector: The Hollywood Reporter, Premier and Variety. "This is a VFX school, not a CG school," Lekuona says, when asked what makes ESCAC distinct from other institutions.

The VFX course offered at ESCAC comprises two three-month modules, a VFX introductory course and a specialised Masters course. In the introductory course, students learn all they need to pursue work as a junior generalist in the industry, experiencing and learning all the elements that go into creating VFX.

Critically, ESCAC has formed a new relationship with the visual effects studio Minimo, which is in the process of basing its studio in Barcelona. "A significant advantage of this is that the students come into direct contact with working professionals, which opens doors into the professional world." Lekuona explains. "We're currently working on getting the best studios to take our students on work experience contracts. In our eagerness to improve we've signed up some of the very best professionals in the field for the VFX school." ESCAC's alliance with Minimo brings together top professionals in the sector from studios such as ILM, Framestore, MPC, Cinesite and Weta Digital.

▶ "Our teachers train their future colleagues," says Aritz Lekuona of ESCAC

Full-length films

In recent years ESCAC has produced full-length feature films such as Eva and Animals. Dozens of ESCAC's students have gone on to establish their own editing, sound, post-production and production studios, and have managed to completely turn the Spanish production scene around.

Indeed, the work of ESCAC's own production company has won over 400 international awards with work produced by its students. The most important include the Silver Sun from the San Sebastián Festival of Cinema Advertising in 2003, the prize for the best international short film at the Sundance Festival 2006, and Radio Television Espanola's Critical Eye award in 2008. ESCAC graduates have collected five Goya awards, Oscar nominations for Student Academy Awards, and Sant Jordi and Golden Reel awards, among others.

Location: Barcelona, Spain
Tel: +34 93 736 15 55

NO SE PUEDE PROGRAMAR
LO QUE SIENTES

DANIEL
BRÜHL

MARTA
ETURA

ALBERTO
AMMANN

CLAUDIA
VEGA

ANNE
CANOVAS

LLUIS
HOMAR

EVA

SITGES 2011

DIRECCIÓN KIKE MAÍLLO

www.evapelicula.com

◄ This student project
sees a CG horse placed
into a live scene

◄ ► ESCAC contributed
effects to the Kike
Maíllo film Eva

We expect:

"Students to work and make an
effort, and to study to become
generalists. In the generalist
courses, we provide students with
the tools they need to know how
a VFX department works"
**Aritz Lekuona,
marketing director, ESCAC**

Graduates of ESCAC include Juan Antonio Bayona (director of
The Orphanage and The Impossible), Eduard Grau (director of
photography on A Single Man and Buried), Xavi Gimenez (director
of photography on The Abandoned and The Machinist) Kike
Maillo (director of Eva) and many, many more.

When ESCAC students complete their studies, their
relationship with the school doesn't end. The school works with
various organisations to provide free ongoing training for its top
students. Some of the most outstanding examples of student
accomplishment are Lluis Castells and Alex Vilagrasa, who can
number among their achievements the biggest and highest-
earning Spanish films in recent years: The Orphanage, The
Impossible, Julia's Eyes, and the REC trilogy.

Applications to the school should be made by email
(**vfxschool@escac.es**). Send ESCAC your application form, a
CV and a letter explaining why you want to study with it.

"We're different from other schools," Lekuona concludes.
"Our courses are designed to create artists, not graduates.
We give our students the knowledge, the confidence and the
right experience for success in the professional world." ●

◄ "Our courses are
designed to create
artists," says Aritz Lekuona

DAVE School

daveschool.com

DAVE School offers students a vibrant creative environment in which to learn the craft of animation and visual effects via its intensive 12-month course

Deciding to step into the brave, new and ever-changing world of computer animation and visual effects is an exciting prospect. In pursuing your filmmaking, animation and visual effects ambitions, there are technological skills and aesthetic rules to be understood that will enable you to achieve memorable and vivid images in your portfolio of work.

The Digital Animation and Visual Effects School (DAVE School), based on the backlot at Universal Studios, Orlando, Florida, is now in its eleventh year of delivering a high-calibre, leading-edge student experience. The school offers a single 12-month course, at the end of which graduates receive a diploma in Digital Animation and Visual Effects. (A 10-week boot camp in using Maya is also available.) Martin Knapp, creative director at DAVE, explains why the course offers students an advantage. "Its short programme length and intensity mean from start to finish students will spend just 12 months at the DAVE School. This creates an environment which feels more like a real studio, where the tools you learn are what you'll be using every day once you're in a studio.

"Our students appreciate the intense year of high-level education they get when they come to our school, in comparison to spending three to four years somewhere else where they learn only half of what we teach. Every second our students spend at our school is dedicated to teaching the real-world tools that studios are looking for in new hires."

Some of the movies and TV shows that DAVE graduates have worked on include Avatar, The Expendables, Gulliver's Travels, Beowulf, Jackass 3D, Lost, Fringe, 24 and Battlestar Galactica. A member of the Visual Effects Society, DAVE educates its students in the various related disciplines that make up animation and visual effects production for the increasingly convergent worlds of film, TV and computer gaming.

What you learn

At DAVE a typical class consists of 20 to 30 students, with 40 students being the maximum. The college takes pride in its 10:1 student to tutor ratio, which allows for consistent and thorough feedback to be given to students.

The learning experience is built around regular classes that are taken in the Learning Lab, where each student has a workstation. DAVE's resources are extensive and include an 11,000 square foot greenscreen studio, mo-cap studios and stereoscopic technologies.

Throughout their studies at DAVE there are numerous opportunities for students to engage in the professional practice of collaboration with each other, project analysis and reviewing work in progress and work completed in order to take lessons on one project through to the next. All through their course, students also attend classes in film studies to learn from the traditions of moviemaking and put their own work in context.

The course at DAVE is structured around four subject area blocks, each block being a term of around 300 hours of study time. First up is digital modelling and texturing. This block leads to a focus on the fundamentals of computer animation – rigging, posing, facial mo-cap and animation for computer gaming. Phase three then enables you to transfer many of the skills you learn in the first two blocks into the realm of visual effects, and finally the fourth block of study gives students the opportunity to work with stereoscopic 3D.

Significantly, students are encouraged to develop a wide range of skills and capacities in VFX and animation, rather than specialising in particular areas of these disciplines too soon. The impulse here is to equip students with a diverse skill-set that should offer them more opportunities as they venture into the worlds of film and gaming content production. The college's prime location means DAVE is readily able to provide connections and support for students in terms of industry placements.

DAVE enjoys a range of student successes on high-profile projects. Alumni include Amy Putrynski, who went on to become a VFX supervisor at Worldwide FX; Dean Lewandowski, who works as a layout technical director at Weta Digital; John O'Mahony, an environment artist at Vigil Games; and April Warren, a mo-cap lab supervisor at Digital Domain.

So, if you want to make an application to DAVE and get your dream of working in animation and visual effects rolling in the

Location: Orlando, USA
Tel: +1 407 224 3283

► DAVE School offers greenscreen, stereo 3D and mocap facilities

We expect:

"Student success requires personal dedication that goes way beyond our programme. It's not enough to simply attend and participate. You have to be willing to work hard. You must strive to grow as a craftsman, a storyteller, and an artist"
Steve Warner, executive director, DAVE School

◄ Filming a combat scene in DAVE School's greenscreen studio

► On the set of Nazi Robots, a recent student production

◄ Students learn the nuts and bolts of CG in just 12 months

real world, what do you have to do? First, prospective students need to provide proof of a high school diploma or equivalent. If an applicant is under 18, then he or she must provide written consent from his or her parent or guardian. Applicants are expected to have basic computer and internet skills and should be ready to respond to DAVE's request for a Sample of Creativity, which could range from a short film project to a short story or a digital photograph. The answer's in the question, of course: show them your creative energy.

Finally, taking a course at DAVE is about more than just the 12 months you spend studying at the college. "If you ask any of the students here at the school, they would likely say that what really appeals to them is the level of community feel here," says Knapp. "All of our instructors and staff care greatly about what happens after you leave the DAVE School. We're not just concerned about how you do when you're in the programme. Our priority is to prepare you for a job in the industry, which is why we form so many connections with studios all over the world and work closely with each student to make sure they're placed in major studios, game companies, and ad agencies." ●

◄ Team productions from DAVE students include The Solo Adventures

Clik Clak (Fréchinos/Moulin/Wagner)

Hezarfen (Ari/Blanchet/Huang/Hurlin)

Puss in Boots (alumnus Chris Miller, director) Copyright © DreamWorks/Paramount

Supinfocom École d'Animation

Valenciennes and Arles, France

Contact: supinfocom@ndf.cci.fr
+33 327 284 353
Website: supinfocom.fr

Key courses:
● Foundation Animation (*3 years*)
● Advanced Animation (*2 years*)

T he Supinfocom school of animation is widely regarded as one of the best in the world. The school has a reputation in the 3D animation sphere that's unmatched by just about any other institution. Established more than 20 years ago, Supinfocom prides itself on its aims to instil a passion for beautiful images and a taste for narration. With two campuses in France, the school has also recently expanded with a new media building in India. All locations offer a three-year foundation course in animation, which can be extended by a further two years with the advanced programme. The faculty consists of working professionals, who teach in world-class facilities featuring the latest technology. Supinfocom also has a new Digital Greenhouse building planned (to be completed by September 2013), which among other things will feature a 450-seat amphitheatre with 3D projection.

CalArts California Institute of the Arts

California, USA

Contact: admissions@calarts.edu
+1 661 255 1050
Website: calarts.edu

Key courses (undergraduate):
● BFA Experimental Animation (*4 years*)
● BFA Character Animation (*4 years*)

Key course (postgraduate):
● MA Experimental Animation (*3 years*)

E stablished in 1961 by Walt and Roy Disney, CalArts has a long-standing international reputation for excellence in animation production. CalArts educates the next generation of professional artists in a learning environment founded on excellence, experimentation, critical reflection and independent enquiry. Programmes in experimental and character animation are offered, both of which include training in 3D CG as well as other areas, such as 2D techniques and animation history. With first-class facilities, the latest technology and strong ties to companies such as Pixar and Disney, students are exposed to comprehensive curricula using the most up-to-date tools and techniques of the industry. Both programmes welcome regular guest speakers, some of whom are the school's alumni, including Tim Burton. The school also runs annual portfolio days, which are attended by representatives from the major animation studios.

A Travers la Brume (Boubounelle/Bhatt/Gauthier/Girard/Guibot/Voisin/Xia)

Blind Spot (Bessiere/Chauvelot/Clert/Dubois Herry/Jardel/Rouby)

Full Sail

Florida, USA

Contact: +1 407 679 0100
Website: fullsail.edu

Key course (undergraduate):
■ BSc (Hons) Computer Animation

Full Sail has offered students innovative training for the entertainment industry for over 30 years. Still at the top of its game, Full Sail offers a comprehensive and immersive project-based course. The goal of the programme is to provide students with the knowledge and understanding needed to gain entry-level industry positions as technical directors, character designers, lighters and renderers. Full Sail's courses are based on a 'real world' education structure, meaning students generally work between 8-12 hours a day, just as they would in the industry.

The campus is equipped with world-class studios and production spaces, which are often used by companies for real productions. The faculty is made up of veterans of the industry, many of whom still work on professional projects as they teach. The school also integrates guest speakers into the training course. Full Sail's advisory board includes members from Sony Pictures Imageworks, Digital Domain, Critical Mass, ILM and Blue Sky Studios.

USC School of Cinematic Arts

California, USA

Contact: admissions@cinema.usc.edu
+1 213 740 8358
Website: cinema.usc.edu

Key courses (undergraduate):
■ Minor in Animation & Digital Arts (*varies*)
■ BA Animation & Digital Arts (*4 years*)

Key course (postgraduate):
■ MA Animation & Digital Arts (*3 years*)

The USC School of Cinematic Arts is widely recognised as one of the most prestigious film schools in the world, which is no surprise considering the likes of George Lucas and Robert Zemeckis studied there. In the last 15 years, the two legendary directors have separately donated huge amounts of money to expand the school – funding the addition of the Robert Zemeckis Centre for Digital Arts and the George Lucas Instructional Building. The facilities on campus at the USC are world-class, with software and hardware that would put many visual effects studios to shame.

The school offers both undergraduate and postgraduate training courses in animation, which are four and three years in length respectively. Courses are taught by faculty members who either are or have been working professionals and so constantly expose students to the changing trends in the industry.

Gobelins L'Ecole de l'Image

Paris, France

Contact: +33 140 799 279
Website: gobelins.fr

Key course (undergraduate):
■ Diploma in Animation (*3 years*)

Highly respected in the world of animation, visual effects and games, Gobelins L'Ecole de l'Image is putting France on the map as a place to go for a world-class education in the arts. Operated by the Chamber of Commerce and Industry of Paris, it offers both basic and professional training in many areas, including digital and 3D animation. Founded over 35 years ago, the school's animation department is constantly evolving to prepare artists with the growing needs of the animation industry. Almost all the Gobelins teaching staff are working professionals, and the school attracts animation artists, directors and producers from around the world as guest speakers.

The three-year animation programme builds on the traditional curriculum, focusing on both hand-drawn and digital techniques while nurturing the student's creativity. By the end of the diploma, animation students will have created a short film, which serve as the openers at all the official screenings of the International Animated Film Festival in Annecy, France.

Gobelins encourages students to get involved in internships during the holiday periods in animation studios and production companies. The school also runs exchange programmes with CalArts California Institute of the Arts in the USA, the Institute of Animation, Visual Effects and Digital Postproduction at Filmakademie Baden-Württemberg in Germany, and The Communication University of China in Beijing.

Insun Kwon

Our cover image is by Insun Kwon, a 3D character artist and SCAD MFA student in animation. Trained as a a traditional sculptor, Insun moved to digital modelling in 2008. He is currently finishing his thesis film, 'Nature of Life'
insunkwon.com

IN ASSOCIATION WITH

SCAD. The University for Creative Careers®

ATLANTA   HONG KONG   LACOSTE   SAVANNAH   eLEARNING

3D
WORLD

Showcase
The month's best new commercial 3D projects

South African studio DXF
Extreme Effects used
ZBrush to create forms for
its campaign for Aquartz
Natural Mineral Water

Projects

This month's round-up of commercial work includes a world of water, a winter wonderland and a trip down memory lane

◄ Project: **Aquartz**
Studio: **DXF Extreme Effects**

This refreshing water world was created by South African studio DXF Extreme Effects for Aquartz – a product of the country's food and drinks group Clover. The studio heard about the project after being approached by advertising agency Joe Public. Keen to get onboard, the DXF team created some test renders, which won them the pitch. The team was then responsible for the entire digital creation of the images, including 3D modelling, lighting, rendering, retouching and grading.

DXF created rough base meshes of all the 3D elements in Maya, then exported them into ZBrush and recreated them using the ZSphere system. The team used ZSketch tools to build the forms, and to detail finer displacements at the end of the process. Finally, DXF used Maxwell for rendering and Photoshop for retouching, grading and comping.

Although the ad was put together with a combination of software, it was ZBrush that proved the most useful on the project. DXF Extreme Effects owner Wayne Troskie explains: "ZBrush was the main tool used to create the water world. I tried various water applications, which are based more on physically accurate simulations, but I needed something more customisable. Something where you could move and blend drops into each other. ZBrush's sculpting tools were amazing throughout the project."
dxf3d.co.za

◀ **Project: Quicksilver**
Studio: MOTYW

Poland-based 3D visualisation studio MOTYW created these winter scenes for a recent project for Quicksilver. The studio got involved after being contacted by French architecture firm Nadau Lavergne, which needed a 3D model of the project in its early stages. MOTYW was also responsible for assisting the architects while choosing materials and shapes for the key elements of the building.

MOTYW used 3ds Max for modelling, V-Ray for rendering and Photoshop for post-production. The team also used some third-party plug-ins for 3ds Max, such as MassFX to create the rock wall and SnowFlowPro to create the weather, both of which proved extremely useful on the project.

MOTYW owner Paweł Podwojewski explains: "We had to figure out how to create a good-looking stone wall covered with steel mesh. We started with displacement maps, but the results weren't good enough (especially for close-ups). After several tests with MassFX, we finally managed to render objects that were similar to the reference photographs sent by our client. The geometry was very heavy at that stage, and we came back to good old manual modelling to create five different rock 'panels'. Placing them randomly, we finally achieved the desired result with decent rendering times."

motyw.info

■ **Project: Kuwait TV**
Studio: Infofillers & AI Productionz

This rebranding project for Kuwait TV was a co-production between creative agency Infofillers and Dubai-based studio AI Productionz. The new design was to be centred on Kuwaiti culture, as well as its wildlife, using Arabic calligraphy. Dividing the work, AI Productionz handled the development of the concept, eight 15-second fillers, and the logo. Infofillers was responsible for a four-minute animation sequence titled 'Athan'.

To create the intricate effects, the teams used a combination of Softimage, Maya, mental ray and After Effects. "Treating Arabic calligraphy created the biggest challenge because the polygons are heavy. It's all animated, and for some shots we had hundreds of animated instances," says AI Productionz director Wissam Altroudi. "We used simple deformation wherever we could until our team developed a custom ICE tree that deforms any geometry on another surface based on normal and UV maps."

Third-party plug-ins were also used to help achieve the unique visual style. Infofillers founder Firas J Ershead explains: "The 'Athan' sequence was less complicated because the geometry and rendering depended on a low-poly environment, but the moment I needed to duplicate animated instances – floors, grass, and so on – I realised how slow the scenes will be. Peter Shipkov's SOuP plug-in saved me with its timeShift node, allowing for an easy outMesh to inMesh with a specific time shifting."

infofillers.tv & aiproductionz.com

▲ Project: **Spectrum**
Studio: **Art & Graft**

London-based animation and live-action studio
Art & Graft was responsible for this short film aiming
to teach people about the work of the charity
Spectrum – a provider of autism services based in
Cornwall. Having seen one of the studio's previous
branding projects, Spectrum contacted Art & Graft
directly about working on a project to tell its story.

Art & Graft handled the script, production, design,
direction, illustration and animation of the film.
The project would mix 3D, 2D and hand-drawn
elements, so the team chose Cinema 4D for the 3D
elements and used compositing package After
Effects to pull it all together.

Creative director Mike Moloney explains: "Our
intention from the start of the project was to add 3D
sequences throughout the piece, but we wanted to
make them feel very much a part of the illustrative
style that we'd developed, rather than stand out as
obvious 3D work. We projection-mapped illustrative
elements (hand-drawn brush strokes and line art)
onto our 3D models so that they sat together with
the illustrative aesthetic, but were able to give us
much more depth and movement to the sequences.
The section in the film where we see the blue-print
plans was all modelled and animated in 3D and then
rendered with a sketch shader to match the look of
the hand-drawn illustrations."
artandgraft.com

▶ Project: Virgin Money
Studio: The Mill

It's a trip down memory lane for the Virgin brand in this latest spot, which aims to highlight how far the company has come in the last 40 years. Behind the ad's many CG elements was the team at The Mill, which was responsible for all the VFX elements that couldn't be achieved in-camera, including 3D, 2D, and extensive pre-viz work.

To manage the workload, the team used Maya, mental ray and ZBrush for all the 3D elements. "We couldn't have created the pound coin without the detailed sculpting abilities of ZBrush," says 3D artist Jonathan Wood. "The use of Decimation Master to crush down incredibly large numbers of polygons that we could then load straight into Maya without playing around with displacement was very useful."

The team also used the hardware on set. "We used Spheron cameras to record the lighting setups. This really paid off when we found that sequences originally intended to be live-action shoots became 3D," says Wood. "It meant that we could get the look and feel of the live-action shoot very quickly."
themill.com

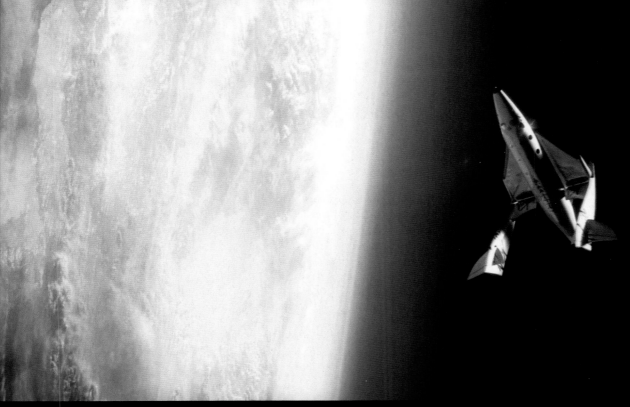

Submit a project

If you would like to see your studio's work featured in these pages, email us at the address below, including brief technical details and at least three print-resolution stills. Please note that we can only feature commercial projects released to the public within the last few months.
enquiries@3dworldmag.com

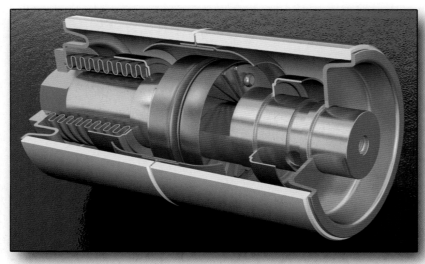

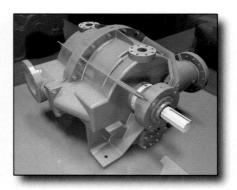

3D WORLD Training

Antony Ward's tutorial reveals how to create working tank tracks using MEL scripts

072

090

088

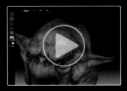
078

Everything you need for our tutorials

ON THE DISC
Videos for ZBrush, Blender and After Effects Q&As, and this issue's Fundamentals tutorial
Disc contents: see page 112

ON THE WEB
All remaining tutorial videos and scene files are on the 3D World website
3dworldmag.com/154

Our guarantee of quality

All of our tutorials are written by experts from the world's leading studios. To ensure their instructions are easy to follow we work through each one ourselves, and you'll find all the supporting files on the disc or online. If you get stuck, just refer to the bonus video walkthroughs provided with most tutorials

Over six hours of video training with this issue →

**Video Guide
Maya
Rigging**

FOR
Maya

ALSO REQUIRED
Silo

TIME TAKEN
10 hours

TOPICS COVERED
- Low-polygon modelling
- Subdivision surface modelling
- Hard surface modelling
- Vehicle modelling
- Maya expressions
- MEL scripting

ON THE WEB
- Video tutorial
- Scene files
3dworldmag.com/154

About the author
Antony Ward has been developing games since the early 1990s. He's worked for some of today's top game studios, and has written three books and numerous tutorials for magazines and websites
ant-online.co.uk

Rig tank tracks in Maya

Antony Ward reveals how to use Maya expressions to create an easy-to-use rig

Whether it's characters or vehicles, animals or scenery, every project you embark on will need a different approach when it comes to rigging your models. Your subject will need to move in a certain way or have unique attributes to take into account, for instance. But above all else, the rig must be easy for the animator to use.

In this project, I'm combining both character and vehicle rigs as I look at creating Bob-Bot, a robot with arms, a head and tank tracks for feet. I'll be focusing on the tank tracks rather than the other components, creating a fun little rig that will automate the movement of the tracks, and adding some basic functionality.

Initially, I'll glance over the modelling of the robot and the tracks in Silo before jumping into Maya. Here, I'll use a series of expressions to drive the tracks around the three main wheels. Using this approach will give the animator more freedom and flexibility because the tracks will move naturally as the wheels move, rather than their movement being dependent on the Time Slider.

Stage 1

Building the wheel and tracks
The first video tutorial for this project is a compressed time-lapse, squeezing a few hours of work down to about 15 minutes; but it should be a good enough guide to get you started. What follows is a more focused recording of the wheel and track creation, which is the focus of this tutorial, and is where we jump in. You can watch the complete build in the first two videos as an added bonus.

⏸ Video 2 00:05
Build the wheels
To create the models you use subdivision surfaces. These enable you to create simplistic proxy models that you can smooth, making the model appear more complex, but without increasing the actual density of the mesh. For the wheels you begin with a basic cylinder. With the help of the Split Poly, Extrude and Bevel tools, you're quickly able to achieve a more detailed appearance.

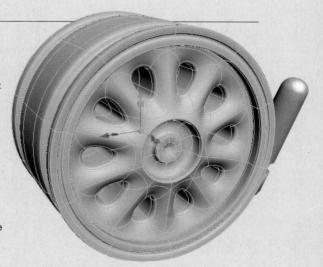

◪ **Video 2** 00:05 Rework a basic cylinder with the Extrude tool to form the main wheel model

◀ Rig the tank tracks for this robot with Antony Ward's guide

103 MINUTES
OF VIDEO

Follow Antony Ward's modelling and rigging video tutorials
3dworldmag.com/154

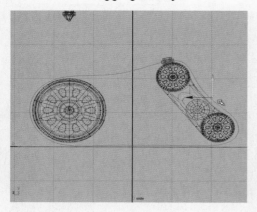

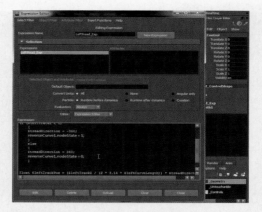

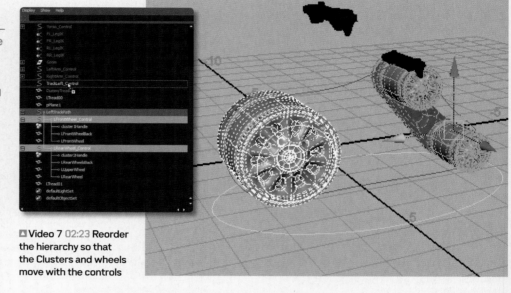

☐ Video 7 00:05
Create Clusters to help animate and deform the path the track follows

☐ Video 7 09:03
Add a Reverse Curve Direction node so the track doesn't flip over

Stage 3

Add path movement, repeat and complete

You're close to finishing the main controls for your first piece of track. The good news is that once you have one working, you can easily adapt the expression to add the remaining pieces. What you'll do first is add a bit more control to the path the tread follows, and then you'll add a fix to the track movement in negative space. With that done it's just a case of adding the other 36 pieces of track.

▐▐ Video 7 00:05
Create Clusters for better path control

It would be ideal if the wheels could move independently on the rig, and when they do, they deform the path the track takes. To do this you can select the affected Control Vertices on the curve, (right-click and select Control Vertex) and then put them into a Cluster (Create Deformers > Cluster). This will give you a small C icon, which now takes control of the Control Vertices, allowing you to animate them, which will in turn deform that section of the path.

▐▐ Video 7 02:23
Edit the hierarchy

With the Clusters created, you can now parent them to the appropriate elements, which will control the wheel movement. In this case you'll add them to the LFrontWheel_Control and LRearWheel_Control so that when you move these icons, the clusters will also move. This also means that the main path you use – LeftTrackPath – can't lie under the TrackLeft_Control icon. Because it's now controlled via the Clusters, parenting it to the main control gives it twice the offset when animated, so it will move off in front of the rig.

▐▐ Video 7 09:03
Tackle the reversing track

Now that the Clusters are in place, it gives you some history on your curve, which also means you can add a new node to stop the track reversing its direction when you pass over the dreaded 0 threshold.

You'll notice that Maya crashes at 10:47 in the video as I work through this. This rig usually works fine, but if yours crashes like mine did, remove the curveInfo node on your path and update the expression with just the actual curve length value.

Select the main curve path – LeftTrackPath – and go to Edit Curve > Reverse Curve Direction. This will add a reverseCurve node to your path, changing its direction. You can use this in your expression to change how the curve acts when it goes past 0. There's already a section that checks for a negative position, so let's include this in the same section. Make the following changes to the expression, again, adding the sections that are highlighted in bold text:

☐ Video 7 02:23 Reorder the hierarchy so that the Clusters and wheels move with the controls

```
int $treadDirection;
float $treadSpeed = 57.5;
float $leftTrackZ = TrackLeft_Control.translateZ;
float $leftCurveLength = curveInfo1.arcLength;
if ($leftTrackZ < 0)
    {
        $treadDirection = -360;
        reverseCurve1.nodeState = 0;
    }
else
    {
        $treadDirection = 360;
        reverseCurve1.nodeState = 1;
    }
float $leftTrackPos = ($leftTrackZ / (2 * 3.14 *
$leftCurveLength)) * $treadDirection;
motionPath1.uValue = ($leftTrackPos %
$treadSpeed)/$treadSpeed;
```

Note that you may also want to directly connect the reverseCurve.nodeState attribute to each Motion Path's Inverse Front attribute, because the track may also flip when it passes 0.

▐▐ Video 8 01:10
Time to repeat

The first section of track is attached and moving around the path. What you need to do now is add the remaining 36 pieces. Don't worry – you won't need to go through this whole process again for each one!

Duplicate the track model and attach it to the path, as you did before using a Motion Path. On the new Motion Path node Break Connections on the uValue attribute. You don't need to add a new expression because you can simply add another line to the current one, telling it to do the same as it has

before, but also affecting the new Motion Path. Make the following changes to the expression, adding the sections highlighted:

```
int $treadDirection;
float $treadSpeed = 57.5;
float $leftTrackZ = TrackLeft_Control.translateZ;
float $leftCurveLength = curveInfo1.arcLength;
float $treadOffset = 1.5;
if ($leftTrackZ < 0)
    {
        $treadDirection = -360;
        reverseCurve1.nodeState = 0;
    }
else
    {
        $treadDirection = 360;
        reverseCurve1.nodeState = 1;
    }
float $leftTrackPos = ($leftTrackZ / (2 * 3.14 *
$leftCurveLength)) * $treadDirection;
motionPath1.uValue = ($leftTrackPos %
$treadSpeed)/$treadSpeed;
motionPath2.uValue = (($leftTrackPos +
$treadOffset) % $treadSpeed)/$treadSpeed;
```

As you can see, you've included a $treadOffset variable so the model isn't in the exact same place as the previous one. If you wanted to continue and add a third and fourth piece of tread, you'd simply multiply the $treadOffset value:

```
motionPath3.uValue = (($leftTrackPos + $treadOffset
*2) % $treadSpeed)/$treadSpeed;
motionPath4.uValue = (($leftTrackPos + $treadOffset
*3) % $treadSpeed)/$treadSpeed;
```

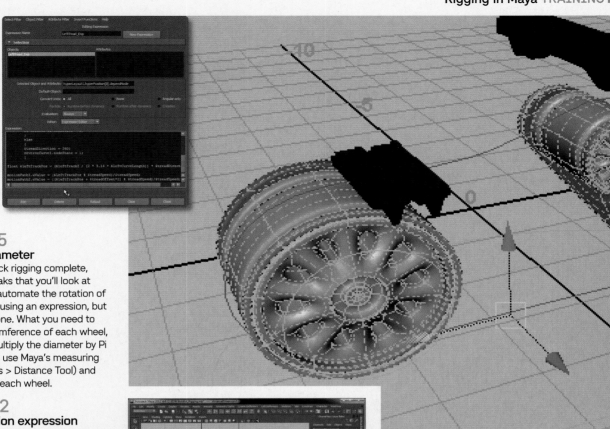

▶ **Video 8** 01:10
With one piece of the track done you can start to create the rest

⏸ Video 9 00:05
Measure the wheel diameter

That should be the main track rigging complete, apart from a few minor tweaks that you'll look at shortly. Your next task is to automate the rotation of each wheel. Again, you'll be using an expression, but this will be a much simpler one. What you need to work out initially is the circumference of each wheel, and to do this you simply multiply the diameter by Pi (3.14). To find the diameter, use Maya's measuring tool (Create > Measure Tools > Distance Tool) and click the top and bottom of each wheel.

⏸ Video 9 01:22
Script the wheel rotation expression

Now you know the diameter, you can create a new expression, similar to the first, but using a slightly modified version of the earlier formula to help you out. The wheel rotation is (Main Control Z Position / (2 * PI * Wheel Diameter)) * 360. So your script should look like this:

```
LFrontWheel.rotateX = (TrackLeft_Control.translateZ
/ (2 *3.14 * 1.885)) * 360;
```

You can duplicate and update this piece of code for all the wheels, so you end up with an expression such as the following:

```
LFrontWheel.rotateX = (TrackLeft_Control.translateZ
/ (2 *3.14 * 1.885)) * 360;
LUpperWheel.rotateX = (TrackLeft_Control.translateZ
/ (2 *3.14 * 0.85)) * 360;
LRearWheel.rotateX = (TrackLeft_Control.translateZ /
(2 *3.14 * 0.85)) * 360;
```

⏸ Video 9 04:25
Add extra attributes

The expressions are done, and you can automate the wheel rotation and the tread movement just by moving the main controller. You can go further, however. With a few simple tweaks you can add even more controllability to the rig. Select the TrackLeft_Control icon, go to Modify > Add Attribute, and add three new float attributes called Track Speed, Track Length and Track Offset. Rather than having solid values coded into the expression, why not open these to the animator too? To do this, simply alter the expression so the $treadSpeed, $leftCurveLength and $treadOffset variables point to the new attributes. Your expression should now look like this:

```
int $treadDirection;
float $treadSpeed = TrackLeft_Control.TrackSpeed;
float $leftTrackZ = TrackLeft_Control.translateZ;
float $leftCurveLength = TrackLeft_Control.
TreckLength;
float $treadOffset = TrackLeft_Control.TrackOffset;
if ($leftTrackZ < 0)
```

```
{
$treadDirection = -360;
reverseCurve1.nodeState = 0;
}
else
{
$treadDirection = 360;
reverseCurve1.nodeState = 1;
}
float $leftTrackPos = ($leftTrackZ / (2 * 3.14 *
$leftCurveLength)) * $treadDirection;
motionPath1.uValue = ($leftTrackPos %
$treadSpeed)/$treadSpeed;
motionPath2.uValue = (($leftTrackPos +
$treadOffset) % $treadSpeed)/$treadSpeed;
motionPath3.uValue = (($leftTrackPos +
$treadOffset*2) % $treadSpeed)/$treadSpeed;
motionPath4.uValue = (($leftTrackPos +
$treadOffset*3) % $treadSpeed)/$treadSpeed;
```

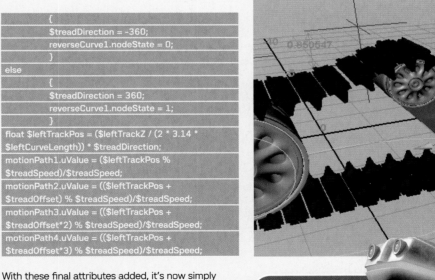

☐ **Video 9** 00:05
Measure each wheel to find its diameter with the built-in tool

☑ **Video 9** 01:22
The expression to drive the wheels is short and simple

With these final attributes added, it's now simply a case of cleaning up the scene, locking off any controls that the animator shouldn't have access to and, of course, creating the track for the right-hand side of your robot. You'll find the completed rig (BobBot_Rigged.mb) in this tutorial's scene files for you to refer to and play around with, but do try to build your own rig from scratch – and that includes manually typing in the code. Cutting and pasting it will be much quicker, naturally, but you'll learn a lot less that way. Also, be sure to watch the videos for a more in-depth tutorial. ●

Expert Tips
Maya
Games

FOR
Maya

TOPICS COVERED
• Character rigging

ON THE WEB
• Reference
  screenshots
  3dworldmag.com/154

20 character rigging tips for game artists

Rigging brings your character's skeleton to life. **Antony Ward** shares his tricks for making the process easier and creating optimal workflows

In most cases, the creation of a character is just the beginning. Once the pushing of polygons and polishing of pixels is over, the model is then passed on to the technical animator, whose role is to give this lifeless bunch of triangles a backbone, clavicles and eventually a full skeleton.

This is just the start when it comes to the art of rigging. The rig itself is the collection of controls, expressions and icons built on top of the skeleton to help move and pose it in a much easier and intuitive way. Here, I'll share some of the key points to consider when creating a new rig, and also highlight any you should avoid.

01 Know your limits
As with every other aspect of game development, when it comes to building a skeleton you'll have limits to adhere to. These limits are set by the target platform and the game engine you're using, and could mean the difference between a fully poseable hand and a basic two-finger mitten. From the project outset you should be aware of these limits, because they will have a drastic influence over the configuration of the skeleton and how the creature or character animates.

02 Talk to the animators
Before you create your first joint it's a good idea to talk to the animators – they're the ones who will be using the rig, after all. They may prefer a certain setup or may need the rig to do particular things, so it's good to have these requests in mind before you start work.

03 Facial setup
One more element to check is if the character will have facial animation. If so, how will it best be achieved? As a technical animator you may have your preferred methods, but again this will be dictated by the game engine. Will the face be manipulated by joints or morph targets? Either way will work but it's a good idea to know early on so you can plan ahead.

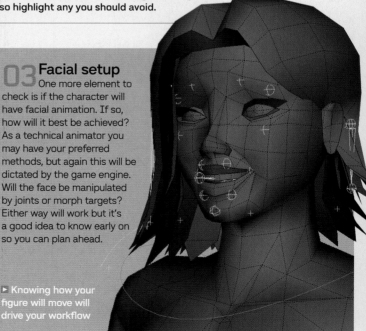

► Knowing how your figure will move will drive your workflow

About the author
Antony Ward has been developing games since the early 1990s. He's worked for some of today's top game studios, and has written three books and numerous tutorials for magazines and websites ant-online.co.uk

◄ Find out how your character will move before starting your rig

04 Check joint positions
The placement of each and every joint is important. Where each is situated inside the model will affect how it bends and moves – each joint is effectively a pivot point, so keep this in mind when building the spine, for example. You may want to run it towards the back of the torso but this will result in pinching as it bends forwards, so experiment with your placements before you commit.

05 The Insert key
Manipulating joints is part of building a good skeleton, but when you move a joint it also moves everything beneath it in the hierarchy. Pressing the Insert key will let you move the joint independently of the others. This method does have its side effects, however: it doesn't update the joint's rotational axes, so these will need to be fixed afterwards.

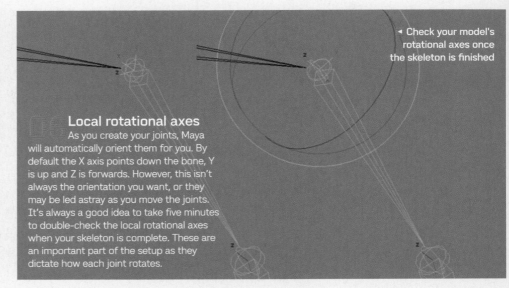

◄ Check your model's rotational axes once the skeleton is finished

Local rotational axes
As you create your joints, Maya will automatically orient them for you. By default the X axis points down the bone, Y is up and Z is forwards. However, this isn't always the orientation you want, or they may be led astray as you move the joints. It's always a good idea to take five minutes to double-check the local rotational axes when your skeleton is complete. These are an important part of the setup as they dictate how each joint rotates.

▲ Changing the Rotate Order can help you to avoid gimbal lock

07 Rotation orders
Another important element to check are your joints' rotation orders. When set up correctly this can reduce the dreaded gimbal lock effect, where two axes become aligned. Prioritise which axis will be used the most and set the order to fit: if, for example, X will be used more during animation, make that the dominant axis under the joint's attributes, meaning it will also move the other two.

08 Time to bind
Connecting the mesh to the skeleton is a simple task, but make sure you use the right configuration. Using a lower Maximum Influences amount and a higher Dropoff Rate will keep the weights tighter to each joint, and make editing the weights easier. Also it's more economical for game engines to have fewer joints influencing each vertex.

09 Painting Weights
The Weight Painting Tool window can seem daunting when you first open it, so initially restrict what you use. Start by blocking out key areas using the Replace Paint Operation while adjusting the Opacity and Value settings. Once you have these in place you can go into more detail with other options, if you need to.

10 Use the Component Editor
Sometimes you need certain vertices to have exact weight values, or perhaps you have an elusive vertex whose weight you can't get right. In these instances you can enlist the Component Editor, which is found under Window > General Editors. If you look under the Smooth Skins tab you'll see a full list of each vertex, and what weight value it has for each joint. You can edit these values to get the exact weights you need.

11 Edit joints after binding
You've attached your skin to the skeleton and painted the weights, but then you notice that you need to tweak the position or orientation of one of the joints. Moving it now will also move the mesh. The best way round this is to use Skin > Detach Skin and make sure you enable Keep History in the options. This will retain your weighting information so that, once edited, you can rebind your skeleton to get back to where you were.

▼ The Smooth Skins tab gives you a useful list of weight values

12 Keep your rig simple

This may seem obvious, but the simpler your rig is to use, the better the animation you'll get from the animators. This doesn't mean you only have to add basic controls: the rig can be as complex as you like under the hood, but on the surface it must be clear and intuitive so the animator can pick up and play. This also means you don't have to train anyone to use it.

13 Use clear icons

Maya has the option to label and display handles for each of your joints, but when faced with 30 identical handles it can be difficult, if not impossible, to tell what you're selecting. Instead use custom shapes, or icons, created from NURBS curves. These are much better to work with and you can make what you like, so the animator can tell instantly what they're selecting.

■ Shapes and icons made from NURBS are easier to work with

14 Consolidate your attributes

Now you have all your icons created, why not do more with them? If you have attributes relevant to that icon – on a blend shape, for example – create new attributes on your icon and directly connect them with the Connection Editor. This way, the animator has all the controls in one place.

15 IK/FK Switch

A fundamental part of any rig is the ability to switch between FK (Forward Kinematics) and IK (Inverse Kinematics). This enables the animator to move the character in a traditional way while also being able to plant and lock feet and hand positions. In Maya it's simple to set up a limb with a controller to switch between both with the help of the Animate > IK/FK Keys menu.

16 Make it unbreakable

Every rig you make should be treated as if it's going into the hands of a child. Lock and hide any attributes that shouldn't be animated or moved. Hide the skeleton and restrict the amount of freedom the animator has when it comes to what they can select, or see. If they place a key in the wrong place the rig will break, which will impact on the schedule and could affect all the animations that have already been done.

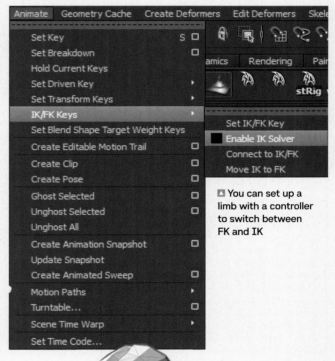

■ You can set up a limb with a controller to switch between FK and IK

17 Add a character set

A character set can be a very powerful tool. It holds all the keyable attributes in one place, making editing animation and transferring it between identical rigs easier. It also opens up a host of powerful tools when you use it with the Trax Editor.

18 Automate the process

Building one rig can be a time-consuming task, so creating a whole set can become a chore. If each rig is set up in the same way, why not let Maya do the work for you? Once you have the first rig you can repeat the task, but this time use MEL/Python to help automate it. Every command is output in Maya's Script Editor, so with a bit of editing you could have a quick script to help with those repetitive tasks.

19 Build additional tools

Don't stop at the rigged character; learn some MEL or Python and start to build tools to help the animators even more. Tools to quickly reverse animations, mirror them or copy and paste poses are all helpful, as are handy user interfaces that allow for quick selection of limbs or body parts.

20 Animate on referenced rigs and keep updating

Rather than using the rigged character directly, suggest that the animators reference a central copy into a new scene before they animate. This way any updates to the rig will happen automatically and seamlessly as, when opened, the scene will bring in the updated rig without the animator even knowing. ●

■ Animating on referenced rigs ensures that characters are updated automatically

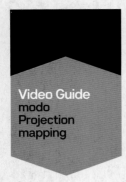

Video Guide
modo
Projection
mapping

FOR
modo 501

ALSO REQUIRED
Photoshop

TIME TAKEN
Two hours

TOPICS COVERED
• Creating an
  HDR image
• Camera projection
• Texturing
• Using the
  Shader Tree
• Render setup

ON THE WEB
• Screen-capture
  video
• Scene files
3dworldmag.com/154

Projection mapping in modo

Mike Griggs explains how to use modo 501's texture-projection capabilities to speed up your modelling workflow

51 MINUTES OF VIDEO

Follow this modo tutorial
using the video walkthrough
3dworldmag.com/154

When you don't have much time to model, but you need to create a realistic textured scene, projection mapping can prove indispensable. This uses images to create realistic 3D models quickly and efficiently. Getting an understanding of projection mapping enables you to focus on modelling and texturing the elements that are important in your scene.

This tutorial shows you how to use the Shader Tree in modo to make a realistic product environment for a look at the potential future of interactive technologies in the home. By adapting a photograph of a piece of furniture, I'll show you how to make a simple HDR texture to create realistic reflections on your objects. Also, I'll show you how to create a 'real' camera projector. I'll then show you how you can use modo's Shader Tree to create luminous transparent textures, as well as how to use one material to texture instances of objects using multiple texture maps.

Stage 01

Create the scene

In the initial stage of the tutorial, you'll create an HDR image to light the scene, as well as set up modo to use plate photography for the background, and define the minimum amount of information you need to create your scene from your reference material. This tutorial is designed for a still image, but I'll also talk about what you need to do to create an animation.

❚❚ Video 1 00:05
Merge the HDR images
To create the environment, I used the Merge To HDR Pro option via File > Automate in Photoshop to bring in shots I took of a reflective ball I placed on the cabinet. I ended up using six of the seven images I imported because the seventh was off-register. The image will be a still, so the final render probably won't veer too far from the camera's position. I only really need one HDR image. If I were going to animate the scene, or radically shift the view, I'd take three sets of exposures around the ball at 120-degree intervals.

About the author
Mike Griggs is a concept designer working across 3D, motion graphics and VFX. He's based in Sussex, UK
creativebloke.com

◩ **Video 1** 00:05 You'll need one HDR image to light the environment of a still, or three if you plan to use animation in the scene

Combine projection mapping with stock meshes to build scenes rapidly when working in modo

▲ Video 1 00:42 Once the HDR is finished, save it as an OpenEXR file to retain all the data

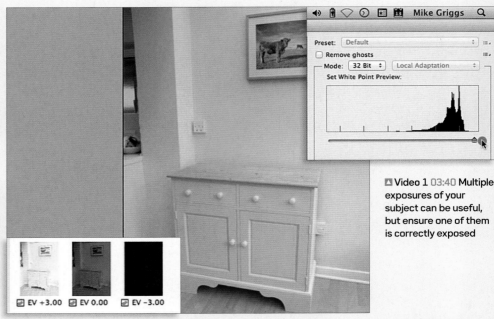

▲ Video 1 03:40 Multiple exposures of your subject can be useful, but ensure one of them is correctly exposed

▲ Video 1 05:04 Set up your scene using precise information from your camera using EXIF data

▶ Video 1 00:42
Finish the HDR image
You now have a 32-bit file that you can test using the slider in the bottom left of the image window to make sure you're happy with the fall-off into both light and dark. I crop as close as I can into the sphere – it doesn't matter if you go slightly over the edges. The sphere captures most of the light behind it as well as in front of it, which makes it excellent for capturing images of this type. Once you finish cropping, fill the areas around the sphere with a neutral colour, such as white, then save the file as an OpenEXR, which keeps all the image data.

▶ Video 1 03:40
Create the backplate
To create the backplate, I used the Merge command to merge three exposures of the cabinet into one image. This enables greater latitude when setting the exposure. However, this method can run into problems, as it did for me, where some green smearing in the shadows crept into the images (this could have been the result of only using three exposures for the image). If you're shooting in raw format, keep a normally exposed image handy to swap in if necessary. If you're shooting JPEGs, I'd still recommend merging the images for the backplate to increase the colour depth. Convert the image down from 32-bit to 16-bit using Image > Mode, then save it as a TIFF or PNG.

▶ Video 1 05:04
Set up modo
Launch modo and click the render icon in the Shader Tree to size the frame the same as the photo of the scene. Set up the modo camera to use the same focal length as in the photo (you'll find this information in the photo's EXIF data), then go to **dpreview.com**, find your camera body in the database and apply the sensor size to the film width and height fields. These two bits of camera information are critical to successfully creating a projected still image. You can improve the results further by matching the f-stop setting of the camera. If you're creating an animation, you'll need tracking data, so you'll also need to remove any details of lens curvature during the modelling, and then replace it in the final composite.

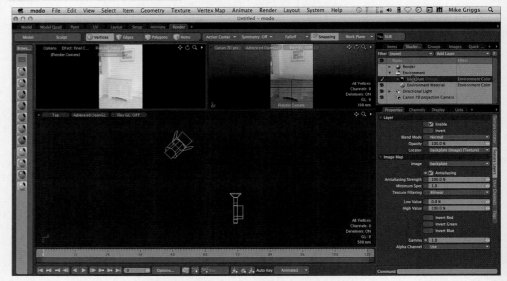

▲ Video 1 07:18 Place the camera in roughly the same position in relation to the cabinet as it was in reality

▶ Video 1 07:18
Add the backplate to modo
Move the camera to its approximate position in relation to the cabinet, and add the scene photograph to the environment in the Shader Tree. Select the image object, which now has the name of the imported image, and in the properties panel, select the Texture Locator tab and switch the drop-down menu for Projector Type to Front Projection. Select the current camera, and the image now appears properly framed in the render view. If you render now, you'd simply get a render of the photograph. Rename the modo camera to something appropriate, because you can use as many cameras as you like as projectors. This can be really useful if you're using this technique on more complex objects and buildings – to give you extra coverage into areas the original photograph doesn't cover.

Stage 2
Modelling using projection mapping
In the second stage I'll create a realistic-looking model using texture maps and a minimum amount of modelling. I'll also look at how to use the HDR imagery you created in stage one to light objects in your scene realistically to match your background image. Finally, I'll show you how to create texture maps of the objects in the background photograph, which can be edited in Photoshop with the perspective removed.

▶ Video 2 00:05
Create the cabinet geometry
Using rough measurements of the real cabinet, I created a simple mesh cube object, which will become the cabinet. If you're inputting the measurements by hand into modo, the object tends to be centred around the world centre point. To set the cabinet to the ground plane, enter the height of the cabinet and then type /2. This tells modo to make the input figure a calculation, and automatically corrects the position of the object, so it's at the right height.

It's worth remembering that you can enter calculations like this into all number input boxes in modo. One way I use the calculation feature, as you'll notice in the video, is to correct the gamma of the imported textures. As a rule of thumb, if you have problems with textures being too light on import, dividing the image gamma by your monitor gamma, in this case 2.2, should fix the problem.

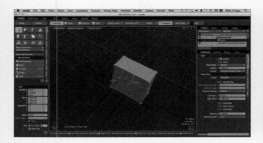

Video 2 00:05 Adding /2 to the height of the cabinet makes the input a calculation

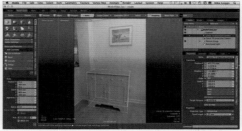

Video 2 01:40 For still images, your projection camera doesn't have to be perfectly positioned

Video 2 04:00 Project the photo onto your basic cabinet mesh to create the projection texture

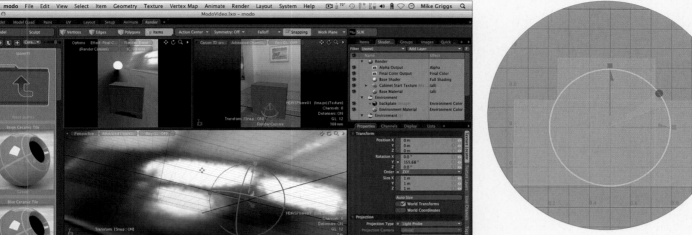

Video 2 05:40 Check the reflection and diffuse properties by placing sphere objects in your scene

Video 3 00:05 Remove the redundant polygons and then bake your texture maps

Video 3 06:40 Build up the sides of the cabinet texture using the Clone Stamp in Photoshop

▣ Video 2 01:40
Position the projection camera
Duplicate the projection camera, then hide it. You now have quick access to the original position if you get lost. Then, using the camera position view in the OpenGL view (set to wireframe), move and rotate the projection camera to a position where you're happy with it. Again, because this is a still image, it doesn't need to be completely accurate. For animation work, you'd need to take a decent set of reference pictures of the camera position as well as a true survey of the camera position and angle on the tripod. Once you have the cuboid in a position you're happy with, apply a material to the object by hitting [M], ensuring you're in Polygon mode rather than Item mode. Applying textures in Item mode can be confusing later in the process.

▣ Video 2 04:00
Create the cabinet projection texture
Switch to the Render tab and make sure the preview is showing the right render output of Final Camera. Expand the Render element, which shows the current render outputs, the Base shader, and the material group you need to create for the cabinet. In the material group add an image layer, again using the photograph of the scene, using the same technique as when applying the image to the environment. This applies the texture of the cabinet to the object as if from a real projector. Select the material object for the cabinet material group and set its diffuse to 100.

▣ Video 2 05:40
Create the HDR environment
Switch off the default Directional Light, go to the Settings tab on the Render object, select the Global Illumination Tab, and enable it. In the Shader Tree,

duplicate the existing Environment object and then set the image in the new environment to the HDR sphere. Set the projection type of the HDR sphere to Lightprobe to enable it to illuminate the scene. In an OpenGL model view, set the background to Environment and disable the original environment so you can see the mapping of the HDR sphere. Orient it to the correct position. Create two spheres of the same size as the real mirror ball and set them on top of the cabinet. Give one ball a mirrored texture and the other an 18 per cent grey texture to check the reflection and diffuse properties of the image.

▣ Video 3 00:05
Bake the texture maps
After creating the geometry for the back wall, use the pen and extrude edge tools to duplicate the cabinet object. Stretch the mesh to ensure you capture all the cabinet from the projection. Make a new UV of this cabinet mesh, and then remove the base and back polygons because they're redundant. Save the UV as an EPS, using Texture > Export UVs To EPS so you have a wireframe of the UV for reference in Photoshop. Going back to the Shader Tree, select the cabinet image in the cabinet material group, right-click and select Bake To File. When this command asks for texture dimensions choose a 4,096-pixel square – this can be downsampled later.

▣ Video 3 06:40
Edit the baked texture
Open the baked texture file in Photoshop, then open the UV EPS and make it the same dimensions as the baked image. Switch off the Antialiased option because it can make the UVs disappear on larger texture sizes. Copy the UV layer into the baked file as a new layer, which enables you to get a representation

of the cabinet geometry on the baked texture. Clone and stretch pixels to approximate the sides of the cabinet. The baked file is a set of elevations of the cabinet, which means you don't have to worry about perspective. Creating correctly flattened images from photos is one of the great advantages of projection mapping, because these can be worked on by team members who don't have to have any 3D knowledge.

▣ Video 3 08:20
Model the final cabinet
Apply a new texture in modo to the UV'd cabinet, and bring in the edited baked texture. To tidy up the cabinet, switch to model view, go to the Edge tab and use the Add Loop command to start adding geometry into the cabinet model. Once you have all the desired loops in place, use the Slice tool to cut any diagonal edges. Delete any polygons on the front face that don't have elements of the cabinet on them. Selecting both sides of the cabinet, cut the polygons and paste them back in. Then with Snap set to Geometry, position the side faces up against the front face. To finish, use the Curve Slice tool in Mesh Edit to cut the curves on the front of the cabinet's base.

»

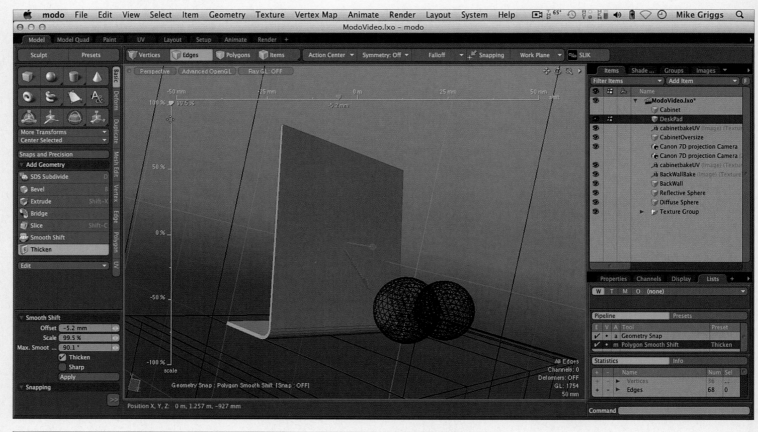

Stage 3

Final modelling and the Shader Tree

In the final stage of the tutorial, you'll look at how to model your futuristic objects and apply graphic transparent texture maps created in Photoshop to these meshes. You'll delve into the Shader Tree to make your graphics pop to life, and you'll also use one material group to drive different objects. Lastly, you'll look at how to create render outputs to generate render passes for your final render.

▮▮ Video 4 00:05
Creating the futuristic objects
Use the same texturing techniques you used for the cabinet on the wall, and then start to create the futuristic objects. To create the computer, use the

Line tool to create a mesh object with two edges, then use the Edge Extend command to create two polygons. Bevel the edge until you're happy with the corner, and then use the Thicken command to add a bit of depth to the computer. Create a texture for the computer and apply one of modo's pre-existing clear plastic textures by dragging the texture from the library directly onto the computer in the Preview window while ensuring that the selection mode is set to Polygon.

▮▮ Video 4 03:00
UVing and texturing the computer
To create the UV for the computer, select the polygon for the screen, move to the UV tab, and delete the UV map that modo created. Make a new UV by right-clicking [new map] in the UV map drop-down

menu. To get the polygon of the computer face on the UV, select Align Workplane To Selection from the Workplane menu in modo's top selection area. This aligns the view to the chosen polygon. Remove all unnecessary polygons in the computer UV model by inverting the polygon selection and hiding them. Click the Project From View button on the left of the screen to create a perfectly flat UV of the slanted computer face. Save it as an EPS as a frame to create the texture for the screen graphics.

▮▮ Video 4 04:25
Apply the design graphics
Complete the graphic for the computer in Photoshop and apply it to the computer mesh by creating an image map in the computer's material group and using the layered PSD of the graphic. By using the PSD, any changes, including transparency, are tracked by modo as you switch and save between the two applications. To make the textures glow, switch the image map from Diffuse Colour to Luminous Amount, by clicking Diffuse Colour in the Effect column of the Shader Tree. Instance the image map, go to the Effect column and switch it from Luminous Amount to Luminous Colour. Using Luminous effects makes textures pop, generating light of their own, which then interacts with other objects in the scene including those with projection maps.

▮▮ Video 5 00:05
Texture the wall panels
The wall panels are a simple cuboid mesh, which you need to instance twice using the same technique you used for the computer to create the texture of the wall panels. This time use Glass from modo's material library, rather than a perspex. Hold down [Shift] and zoom using the mouse scroll wheel into the wall panel in the Preview window to check the texture edges – holding down [Shift] ensures that the camera doesn't

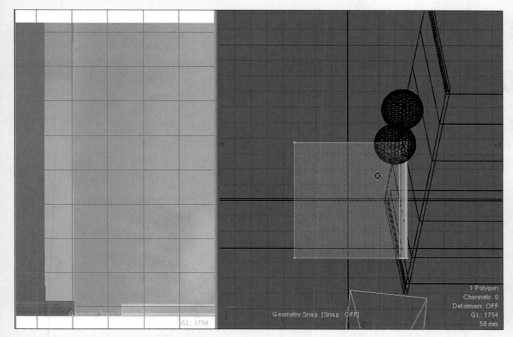

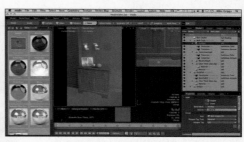

■ Video 4 04:25 Make the computer screen glow using Luminous effects in the Shader Tree

■ Video 5 09:50 Set up your render outputs

■ Video 5 12:25 Save your renders as PNGs as well as OpenEXRs in case the latter corrupt

■ Video 5 00:05 Create the wall panels from a simple cuboid mesh using a glass material

▐▐ Video 5 12:25
Rendering and going further
I render stills as layered OpenEXRs, which I then save as PSDs or 16-bit PNGs. Saving as PNGs ensures you have all the passes easily accessible in case the single EXR corrupts or accidentally gets saved over. To wrap up, this tutorial has shown you the basics of how projection mapping can be used to create realistic objects from photographic references. To take the techniques I've discussed further, try animating the scene by moving the camera around the cabinet. You could also animate the graphics for the computer and wall panels. This can then be imported into modo to make the most of the contact lighting using the excellent modo renderer. ●

move. This is a great way to see details in Preview, such as the blurred edges of a texture's transparency. This is caused by having Antialiasing switched on, which modo does by default. Correct this in the Texture Layers tab of the wall panel graphic in the Shader Tree. Switch Antialiasing off on the computer's texture as well, if you haven't already done so.

▐▐ Video 5 04:55
One material for multiple meshes
The wall panels look great, but they all use the same texture. Two of the three panels are instances, so you can't directly apply a new material to them. Instead, group the image map of the weather graphic within its own logically named (weather) group. With this new weather group selected, go to the Texture Layers tab, select the Item tab, and switch it from (all) to the wall images mesh object. The texture for the two instanced wall panels should disappear in the Preview window. Instance the weather group twice within the wall glyph material group by right-clicking them. Then, use the Item drop-down menu to choose the name

of the two respective wall panel instances. Each instance should now have its own unique weather symbol showing in the Preview window.

Once all the textures are created, drop in a couple of stock meshes from the modo mesh library to add authenticity to the scene.

▐▐ Video 5 09:50
Create the render outputs
By using stock models and projection mapping onto geometry, most creative time has been spent on designing the graphics for the screens, which is the focus of the image. Create a range of render outputs for the scene by right-clicking and duplicating the default outputs of Final Colour and Alpha. Use the render preview to see the result of each render output. Move the computer and wall panel texture above the Base Shader in the Shader Tree. Create a shader and alpha output for both materials to provide dedicated alpha maps. Note that if you place any material group above the Base Shader, you'll need to give it its own shader or it won't render properly.

◄ Video 1 02:29
A shape key stores the position of all the vertices

◄ Video 4
Create top_lip.up and edit the mesh to make Larry sneer

◄ Video 5
Move the outer edge of the eyebrows down to denote worry

Video 2 00:05
Lower face shape keys

Begin by opening start_file.blend from the tutorial files, which contains your unrigged character. There are a few shape keys to make: you'll focus on the jaw, lips, cheeks and eyebrows. If you're using your own character for this tutorial you may also need to add shape keys for the nose and ears. Start with the jaw and work your way up the face.

Before you add the shape keys, go into Edit mode and create left and right vertex groups, and make sure the centre is assigned 50 per cent weight to both groups for a smooth blend.

Create your basis shape key and a new blank shape key: call this **jaw_left**. In Edit mode select the chin, and with proportional editing move it a little to the left relative to the jaw pivot. Repeat this for the right, down and up.

Using videos 3 and 4, start on the lips. Create **smile.L** and edit the mesh to make Larry smile. In Object mode slide the value up to 1, with all other shapes at 0. From the drop menu select New Shape From Mix. Call this new shape **smile.R** and set the vertex groups left and right respectively for these shape keys. Repeat this process for **frown/pout, sneer, cheek-puff, squint, top_lip.up** and **bottom_lip. down**, as well as **F/V**, **O** and **E** mouth shapes.

Video 5 00:05
Teeth, tongue and eyebrows

With the mouth done, you need the teeth to move too. Add two shape keys, **lower.up** and **lower.down**, and edit them respectively. For the tongue you'll create **The** for tongue to teeth, and **ZSL** to move the tongue back for those shapes. With most of the face done, you need some shape keys for the eyebrows.

When you're watching a film or animation you spend a lot of time looking at the character's face, specifically the eyes, so getting your eyebrows to work just right is crucial to conveying the emotions of your character. You not only want to move each eyebrow independently, but you also want to move the inside and outside individually. You'll find that the eyebrows are a separate mesh so you'll require the shapes on Larry and his brows. You'll create inner up and down, as well as outer up and down.

Focus on the shape of the eyebrow during these movements. Inner up is surprised, inner down is angry, outer up is anticipation and outer down is worried. These are the basic emotions you'll be conveying with your eyebrows. By combining these and using different blend values, you can create the full range of emotions.

Stage 2

Rigging your character

Before you can use your character in animation you need to create a rig so you can deform the mesh. Not only will you be creating the base bone structure and weight painting, but with your shape keys you need to learn how to use drivers to allow your bones to control your shape keys.

I'll also cover some simple bone constraints for things like eye tracking, and limits so you don't lose your bones during animation by limiting them to a much smaller area.

Video 7 00:05
Create the base rig

You can now start creating your rig. Add a new armature and position four bones up the spine (base, body, head and hat). Add two bones for the arms/ears and one for the nose. The arms and nose will be parented to the head.

For your eyes, put the cursor at the origin of an eye, add a bone facing directly out (eye parent), duplicate and make a different thickness (lattice parent). Now add a bone stretching to each eyelid (eyelid parent), with another bone at the ends of these (eyelid controller). This is how you'll control the eyelid's rotation around the eye. These will all be parented to the head bone.

To create the look at targets for the eyes, duplicate the eye bones and move them out in front. Add another bone here, and parent the look at bones to it. This will control where the eyes are looking. Add a bone for the upper and lower teeth, the tongue, and a big bone here to parent the teeth and tongue, and parent that bone to the head. This

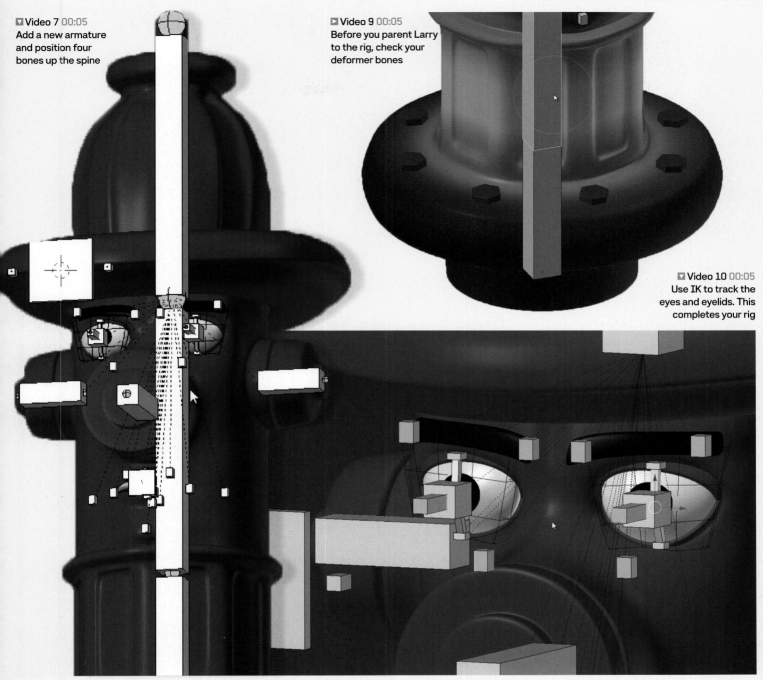

▶ **Video 7** 00:05
Add a new armature
and position four
bones up the spine

▶ **Video 9** 00:05
Before you parent Larry
to the rig, check your
deformer bones

◀ **Video 10** 00:05
Use IK to track the
eyes and eyelids. This
completes your rig

---

will enable you to correct the teeth should they intersect the mesh.

Lastly, add a new bone for each shape key, teeth and tongue. Some shape keys can share a bone, such as smile/frown, chin_up/down/left/right. All these bones will be parented to the head bone. I like to create my face bones on the face itself, while others prefer to have a flat plane of bones to use. It doesn't really matter – if you want to have a flat plane of bones then don't parent them, and move them away from the model. The drivers you'll create will work no matter where they are.

❚❚ **Video 9** 00:05
Parenting and weight painting

Before you parent Larry to the rig, check your deformer bones. In the bone properties, uncheck Deform on any bones that you don't want deforming the mesh directly – shape key bones, all the eye bones and the tongue.

Now select Larry, teeth and tongue, then the rig and parent with armature deform. You'll need to go

in and do some weight painting to clean things up. Weight painting is a long process but you don't have a lot of mesh to work through. Make sure the teeth are only being affected by the teeth bones, and the tongue by the tongue bone, and then move Larry into an odd position. This enables you to see easily what needs correcting. Also parent the eyes to the eye bones and eyelids to the eyelid bones, and parent the bolts to the base bone.

❚❚ **Video 10** 00:05
Limits and Inverse Kinematics

For the bones that are going to control your shape keys, you'll want to apply some limits. In Pose mode, select each shape key bone and add a Limit Location constraint. Set all values to 0, except those where you want it to travel – set these between -0.2 and 0.2. This should give you a good range of movement and yet keep it in place. Make sure you set Convert to Local Space.

The only Inverse Kinematics (IK) you'll be using is for the eyes. You'll use IK to track the eyes to the

look at targets, and also for the eyelids to track to the eyelid controllers. This will complete your rig, so you can move on to the drivers.

❚❚ **Video 10** 05:57
Set up shape key drivers

Split your window and open the Graph Editor. Switch from F-Curves to Drivers – this is where you'll edit your drivers. Back in your object data, right-click on a shape key and select Add Driver. It will now pop up in the Graph Editor. By selecting your rig and the corresponding bone, you can make the bone affect your shape key via the driver. Of course, you need to make a few tweaks. Set the Driver to Averaged Value, the Variable to the correct axis, and Space to Local Space. You can also change the X multiplier to control how far you need to move the bone to control the shape key. Your values for all your drivers will be between 10 and -10.

You now need to repeat this process for all of your shape keys. Check your shape keys to make sure they work how you want them to.

»

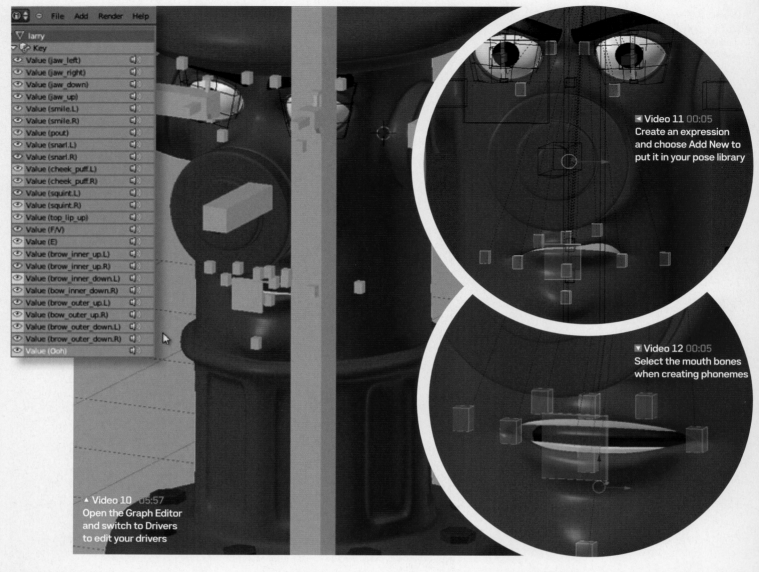

Video 11 00:05
Create an expression
and choose Add New to
put it in your pose library

Video 12 00:05
Select the mouth bones
when creating phonemes

▲ Video 10 05:57
Open the Graph Editor
and switch to Drivers
to edit your drivers

Stage 3

Creating your pose libraries

Instead of creating your pose at every phoneme – which could translate to thousands of times in one clip – you can use pose libraries to make the task incredibly simple.

A pose library is a way of storing the location, rotation and scale of all the selected bones to be called upon at any time. I'll look at how to create a pose library, how to remove elements from it and also how to browse through your poses. I'll focus on a phonemes library, but you can use pose libraries for any pose you wish.

▮ Video 11 00:05
Introduction to pose libraries

The best way to think about pose libraries is that they're like taking a snapshot of the current pose. Let's practise. Create an angry face with your character – incorporate as many bones as you wish (eyes, brows, cheeks and so on). Now select all the bones in the face, excluding the eyes, eyelid_deformers and nose. Press [Shift]+[L] and then choose Add New. This will add the current pose to the pose library.

Before you do anything else, press [F6] or look in your toolbar [T]: you'll see there are some options: the first is Frame. As pose libraries are stored as an animation on a separate timeline, this is the frame

it's on – effectively ordering your poses. The second is Pose Name. As the title suggests, this enables you to name your pose. Call it **Angry Face**. Create a few more of these: **Grin, Worried** and so on.

To browse the poses in the library, press [Alt]+[L]. This actually brings up the Delete menu, to delete the poses, but it's also the quickest way to see what poses you have in your library.

▮ Video 12 00:05
Create your phonemes library

Now you've had some practice, let's create the phonemes. Although advanced rigs require a lot more phonemes, you'll only be creating the basics. You can hide all bones except the mouth bones for this, as they're the only ones you want to use in your pose library. You'll group them into the basic shapes: A-I, E, U, O, C-D-G-K-N-S-Z, R-Y, F-V, L, Th, M-B-P. Finally, create a Rest pose, with the mouth closed in a rested position.

Something to note is that it's easier to create phonemes if you use a mirror while viewing yourself making the mouth shape. It will assist in creating a much more realistic pose.

Also think about what audio clip this character will be using. Is he happy or sad? You may wish to add two more sets of phonemes for happy and sad to your character. However, Larry's mouth has currently been set up to look annoyed anyway, so that will be perfect for later on. Larry is now rigged and ready to go for animation.

Stage 4

Lip-synching your character

To create a believable animation, you'll probably require realistic lip-synching. This involves animating your character at every syllable, which means a lot of keyframes. This would be painstaking work to do by hand, so you can use your phonemes library combined with keyframe recording to animate your character quickly and realistically to your sound strip. In this video I'll cover how to lip-sync manually while you preview the audio clip. This clip comes from the **11secondclub.com** archives for November 2007. I'm using this one because it gives you a lot of emotion to play with.

▮ Video 13 00:05
Get ready to lip-synch

Before you start lip-synching, you need to set up a few things to assist you. Split your window and load up the Video Sequence Editor. You'll add and position your audio clip in here. You'll also change the end frame to 230 because you don't require any audio after that point.

Now for the real magic. In your timeline, select the Playback menu, and check AV-sync and Audio Scrubbing. This enables real-time playing so that the audio matches your animation and enables audio while you scrub through the timeline. Effectively, this allows you to move very slowly through the timeline

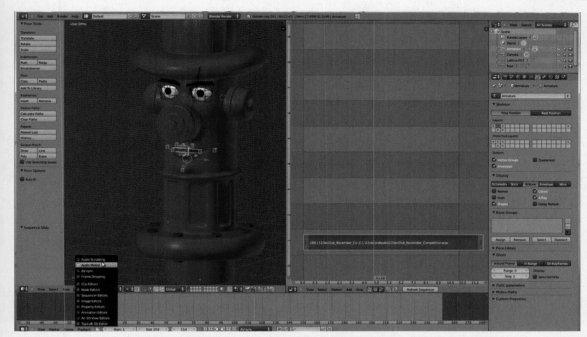

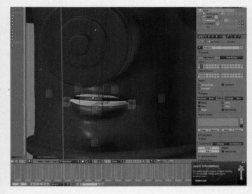

▲ Video 13 04:22 Scrub through the timeline slowly, adding the correct phonemes as you go

so you can pick out each phoneme individually and set the appropriate pose. One final thing to do before you begin lip-synching is to enable automatic keyframe recording. This button is located in the timeline next to the sync mode.

⏸ Video 4 04:22
Lip-synching your character

Now you can begin lip-synching. This is a tedious but simple process. As you scrub slowly through your timeline, use [Ctrl]+[L] and the mouse wheel to select the required phoneme and continue through the timeline. Spend some time on this – as so much focus is on the face, lip-synching needs to be spot on. You'll find you can obtain any phoneme using the ones in the library, or by mixing some together. For example, O and U become Wa, as in 'once'.

Something to keep in mind here is the emotion of the character. You control most of the emotion with the body language and eyes, but some must be done with the mouth too. Larry is obviously upset, so the corners of the mouth will be a little more drooped, and the mouth will remain slightly open and perhaps even quiver slightly during the pauses. If you made an extra set of phonemes for sad expressions, you'll find this step a lot easier.

Continue this process through your audio clip. You can hear he gets more agitated towards the end – you need to account for this, so make the phonemes closer together and more abrupt, as if he's spitting the words slightly.

⏸ Video 14 00:05
Tweaking and blinking

Larry is speaking the lines fine, but you may have noticed that when you playback he seems to skip some syllables. This is normal. Blender has trouble moving all those shape keys in real time, so it skips some. When you render out your scene you'll have a perfectly functioning animation. Now you get to the not so fun part: the tweaking. You need to edit your animation to perfection. Expect to take at least an hour doing this part.

If you'd like to make Larry more sad but didn't create the sad phonemes library, you can actually remove all the keyframes from the smile bones, and make them permanently sad. This is not so good for real people, but for cartoon Larry this will work fantastically as a quick shortcut.

Now you have a few words that you need to take a quick look at. Near the end your character is getting a bit agitated – this is shown through

his voice accenting words such as "short" and "fat". You need to account for this by drawing out the SH and F, as if they're being forced.

My last tip is to select the eyelids, clear location ([Alt]+[G]) and add the pose to the library, only selecting the eyelids. Call this **eyes_open**. Now close the eyes and add this to the library, calling them **eyes_closed**. You can alternate between these to make your character blink.

At the beginning of the animation, the character is feeling depressed, so his blinks will be slow and emotional. At the end he has become agitated, which will result in multiple fast blinks. Have a play around with this, and you can add that extra bit of detail to your animation.

Now that your animation is done, are you ready for a challenge? Test your new skills at lip-synching and animating by entering this month's competition at **11secondclub.com**. You'll be surprised how much you'll learn when you put your skills to the test! ●

Supporting files

ON THE DISC
Videos for the ZBrush, Blender and After Effects Q&As are in the disc's Resources area

Digital reader?
Please visit
3dworldmag.com/claim
to receive your videos

ON THE WEB
Visit the 3D World website for scene files and screenshots
3dworldmag.com/154

Send us a question

No matter what 3D software package you use, our experts are here to help. Send your questions to the email address below and we'll try to find a solution. Include your scene file (no larger than 5MB in size, please) if it helps to illustrate the problem
qa@3dworldmag.com

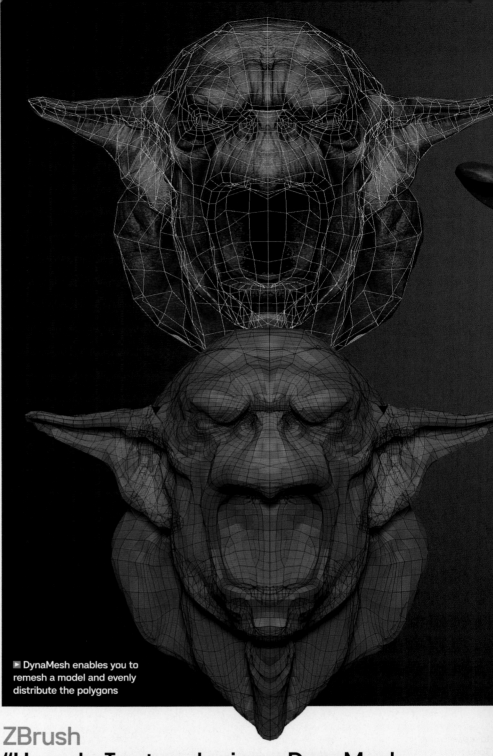

▶ DynaMesh enables you to remesh a model and evenly distribute the polygons

ZBrush
"How do I retopologise a DynaMesh head sculpt in ZBrush?"
Bryan James

Glen Southern replies:

The latest version of ZBrush adds a new tool to its already massive sculpting toolset. DynaMesh gives you the ability to remesh a model and evenly distribute the polygons to prevent stretching. Using DynaMesh you can quickly map out characters and creatures, and try different poses and body shapes in a very small amount of time. The one issue you have is that however fantastic your creation is you may still need to use it in other 3D packages – and you may also require topology that has good edge flow and edge loops. To do that, you need to retopologise the mesh and create a new low-resolution base with the correct topology.

To demonstrate I'll use a DynaMesh-ed orc head. I sculpted it from a primitive 3D sphere and then polypainted it. To retopologise the model, you start off with a basic ZSphere from the Tool palette. Open the Adaptive Skin, Rigging, Topology and Projection palettes. These are the main palettes that you'll use, starting with Rigging.

Select a ZSphere and draw it into the canvas. Make it editable (press [T]) and then go to the Rigging palette. Hit Select Mesh and select the high-resolution head that you want to retopologise. This adds the mesh to the ZSphere, but it may be in an odd position. Using Move mode, reposition the ZSphere so it sits fully inside the head. You may need

Retopologise your mesh in ZBrush

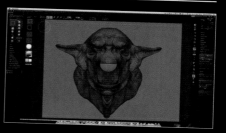

Retopologise with a ZSphere
From the Tool palette, select a standard ZSphere and draw it onto the canvas. Go into the Rigging palette and select your sculpted head mesh.

Lay down new geometry
Begin laying down your new geometry starting from the centre of the model. Activate symmetry with [X] to mirror the geometry on both sides.

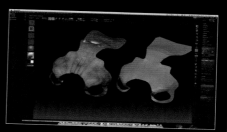

Project more detail
To see more of the detail, increase the Pre-SubDiv slider in the Topology palette to 4. You can also increase the Density slider in the Adaptive Skin palette.

Glen Southern is a 3D artist with over 15 years' experience in film, TV and games. He's owner of Cheshire-based SouthernGFX
southerngfx.co.uk

to resize it as well. In the Topology palette, click Edit Topology and you're ready to lay down your new geometry over the top of your high-res mesh.

This head sculpt is symmetrical and ZBrush enables you to retopologise with symmetry turned on. Hit [X] on your keyboard to activate the symmetry across the X axis. Starting from the top of the head, lay down a line of geometry and then move out across the head. To restart a new line at a new position use [Ctrl/Cmd], and to delete any edges laid in error use [Alt]. Start to add edge loops around the eyes and nose first to give you a good framework of loops to work out from. Keep working around the whole head until the entire sculpture is remodelled with new geometry.

It gets more difficult in areas where you need more geometry or where the mesh is squeezed – for example, the eyebrow corners above the nasal cavity. It's easy to make errors in hard-to-reach places, so it's good to see how things are looking as you go.

If you need to check the mesh, simply press [A] and you'll see that the geometry you've drawn is now visible. It's shown at the base/lowest subdivision level

and there's no surface detail or colour, but it gives a good approximation of your progress. To see what your new mesh would look like with the surface detail projected onto it, you need to use the Projection palette. To make sure the new mesh is showing the higher level of detail, you can increase the Pre-SubDiv slider to 4 in the Topology palette, and increase the Density slider in the Adaptive Skin palette.

Keep trying the preview using keyboard shortcut [A] until you're happy with the results. Once you're ready to conclude the retopology, click the Edit Topology button again in the Topology palette to come out of editing mode. Go to the Adaptive Skin palette and make the head into a new ZTool. Try making it at different levels and see the different amount of extraction you get back.

You now have several meshes from the lowest level of subdivision right up to the highest. To make the most of the polypainting work, you'll need to UV map the mesh either in ZBrush or in a third-party program. You can then convert the polypainting data to a texture map using the new UV co-ordinates, and even extract normal maps and displacement data. ●

nearest to the camera, app... objects further away from the camera blurred and out of focus, or vice versa. With 3ds Max there are

greyscale image. Create a standard camera and point the target at the object you wish to focus on – the object closest to the camera. In the Modify panel, scroll down to Environment Ranges and tick Show. There are two parameters: Near Range and Far Range. Near Range represents the start of the Z Depth and Far Range represents the end. Everything after that will be black. If you adjust them, two planes will slide up and down the camera lens. Set the Near Range to be just after the object you wish to be in focus, and the Far Range to be just after the furthest object you wish to be out of focus. ●

 When saving out your beauty pass and Z Depth, choose a format such as 16-bit colour TIF

James Cutler is founder of MintViz, a creative consultancy providing tutorials, tips and resources for the CG industry
mintviz.com

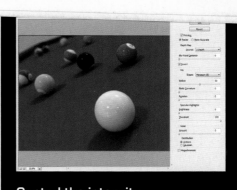

Control the intensity
Control blur intensity by adjusting the radius. Fine-tune position with Blur Focal Distance.

3D WORLD *Reviews*

Software
Renderer

KeyShot 3

The new iteration of Luxion's renderer features an enhanced interface and workflow, and promises better ease of use. **Steve Jarratt** investigates

▶ As long as you have access to CAD files and some HDRIs, making images like this is child's play (lens flares added in post).

PRICE
$995
Upgrade from $395

OTHER EDITIONS
- Pro, $1,995
- Pro Floating Licence, $2,995
- Animation module, $500

MAIN FEATURES
- Real-time interactive HDRI rendering
- Drag-and-drop materials and backdrops
- Animation system based on offset transforms
- Imports a wide variety of CAD formats

DEVELOPER
Luxion

WEBSITE
keyshot.com

Unbelievably, there are people in the world of 3D that don't want to spend their entire lives fiddling with vastly complex shader trees or node graphs. Some people – artists working in the world of engineering, automotive design, product visualisation, jewellery, print illustration, and so on – need to open a model, add some materials and view the end result. Which is precisely what KeyShot 3 does.

In truth, KeyShot has done it since it was called HyperShot and published by Bunkspeed, but this latest iteration adds a new layer of user-friendliness, supports a wider range of formats, and now has the ability to create basic animations, which we'll get to later.

The underlying concept of KeyShot is its real-time renderer, which operates solely using high dynamic range images. There's no complicated lighting set-up required: just drag and drop your HDR image into the scene and your model's lighting, reflections and refractions are all handled

automatically. KeyShot also supports an invisible ground plane to catch shadows so your models appear 'grounded' in the scene. These are accurately cast from bright lights, and they really tie the image into the backdrop. An array of tools enable you to move and rotate the object and alter the location, scale and rotation of the HDR image, so you can frame the scene precisely to your liking.

Key to this new release is a raft of interface tweaks. Improvements to the tool bar, material and content libraries, and an app-wide clean-up of menus and dialogs makes this version a much smoother, friendlier experience. A new library panel shows all the materials

currently in use, while the material editor gains an interactive preview and has been overhauled to reduce clutter, with rarely used controls hidden in an 'Advanced' panel. KeyShot certainly now feels like a much more solid, mature program, and the majority of controls and menus are but a keyboard shortcut away (including the panel that shows you what all the keyboard shortcuts are).

> *KeyShot feels like a more solid, mature program, and the majority of controls and menus are but a keyboard shortcut away*

Of course, the big news for KeyShot users is the addition of the new (and optional) animation system. Based on offset transforms, the system removes the need for keyframing and the inherent complexity this introduces. To facilitate this level of animation, every part of a model can now be moved and rotated, either in world or local space, which in itself is useful for creating static, exploded views of your subject.

CUT-AND-PASTE ANIMATION
To apply an animation, you simply select the part (either on screen or via the Project panel), then create a translation or rotation offset and set the timing. This animation can then be renamed and pasted to any other relevant part – although this has to be done individually rather than on a selected group. If you select Paste Linked Animation, any subsequent changes made to this offset are carried over to all parts with the animation applied.

Tom Kirkup

About the author
Steve Jarratt is an award-winning journalist with two decades of experience. He's also the former editor of *3D World* and a big LightWave enthusiast

▲ With support for depth of field, dispersion and caustics, KeyShot is great for product shots such as this

Roller Reveal video courtesy of Geoff Davies at

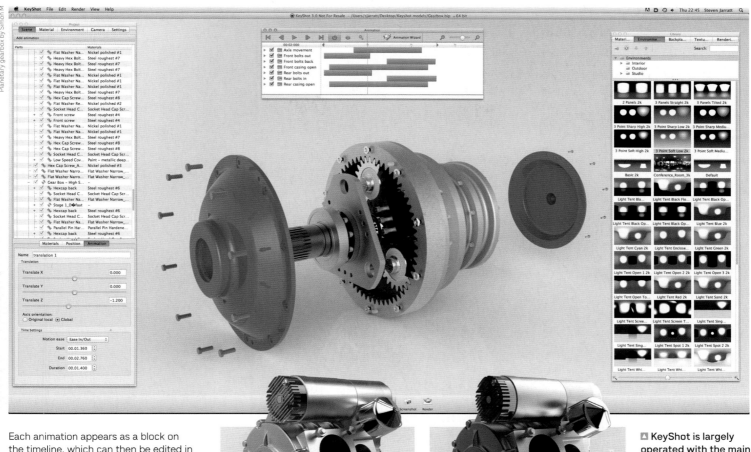

Planetary gearbox by Simon M

Each animation appears as a block on the timeline, which can then be edited in a non-linear fashion; moved to any point in time, and lengthened or shortened to affect its duration. The ability to group animations into folders for editing en masse is a real help when you start accumulating lots of animation blocks across a multitude of parts, but assuming you've organised everything properly, finessing the timing is really very easy.

Because of the way you apply animation offsets to individual parts, the ease of the process is largely reliant on the quality of the structure of your model. Some CAD models imported were simply a list of parts, sometimes with multiple sections to one part, while some were neatly named and grouped. If you have animation in mind, it's best to have your model as organised as possible – you won't thank the modeller when you're animating your 50th bolt of the day.

STILL SOME WORK TO DO
The one feature I'd like to see is the ability to group parts into folders and sub-folders in the Project panel. Parts appear as entries in a list (often a very lengthy one with no real hierarchies), and while these can be [Shift]-selected and have materials applied collectively, it would be far nicer to group multiple items into user-defined folders. You could then apply a material or animation to this folder and have it propagate to the parts within, overcoming the problem of CAD files that arrive with individual parts split into smaller components (or even individual polygons in some cases). Luxion says it's addressing this flaw in the upcoming version 3.1.

Similarly, the addition of nested animations or parent/child links should

be on Luxion's to-do list. If your model doesn't contain a proper hierarchy, it's hard to animate complex interdependent mechanisms using the existing system.

A lot of the quirks and irritations of earlier versions of KeyShot have been removed, and it's now easier and quicker to use, with rapid access to all facets of the program. The speed and quality of its renderer have never really been in doubt, so now you can arrive at top-quality results in even less time. With a suitable collection of HDR images – or an app such as HDR Light Studio, which now plugs right in to KeyShot – generating beautiful-looking, photorealistic renders is stupidly easy. And with he ability to output animations you can present your creations in an even more professional light.

However, you could reasonably argue that the animation system should be an integral part of the upgrade, rather than a $500 option. Indeed, the overall pricing feels a little steep compared with other 3D suites that feature high-quality real-time renderers, plus a variety of modelling and animation tools – the only thing missing from its competitors is the native support for CAD formats that KeyShot has.

So there are a few rough edges in KeyShot 3, and there's still room for improvement in the interface and workflow, especially with complicated, multi-part objects. The animation system also has plenty of room to evolve and expand, too, but this release marks another solid step forward for KeyShot. Luxion adds that you can expect more HDRI controls and and new lights in version 3.1 ●

◢ KeyShot is largely operated with the main interactive render display, the Project window (left), Library (right) and a Timeline if you're producing an animation

◢ You can have a simple flat backdrop colour for your image, while an HDRI provides the lighting. Simply drag in a different HDRI to produce a new lighting scheme

3D WORLD VERDICT

PROS
- Animation is easy to set up and tweak
- Extensive material presets and HDR library
- UI improvements really speed up workflow

CONS
- Complex models can be tricky to organise
- Expensive compared to mainstream apps
- Animation system is quite rudimentary

KeyShot is an absolute doddle to use, and it produces lovely renders, but it relies on models that have been carefully organised

◁ ▽ Finally, the stone-age mental ray integration in Maya gets a worthwhile overhaul with this new plug-in from CoreCG

Software
Maya plug-in

PRICE
Node-locked licence,
$189

OTHER EDITIONS
Floating licence (includes
five render-only
licences), $199

PLATFORM
Windows / Mac OS X /
Linux

MAIN FEATURES
• Node-based render
  pass system
• Ambient Occlusion
  through multiple levels
  of transparent objects
• Large Shader library
  with Material, Texture
  and Utility Shaders
• Python API means you
  can use MentalCore in
  any pipeline
• Colour management
  for sRGB, Linear and
  Rec 709

DEVELOPER
CoreCG

WEBSITE
core-cg.com

MentalCore 1.0

Does the release of MentalCore mean people might stop complaining about mental ray for Maya all the time? **Paul Champion** finds out

MentalCore is an off-the-shelf plug-in for Maya from CoreCG that aims to provide greater efficiency when working in mental ray. It integrates tightly into its host, augmenting the shading, lighting and rendering workflow. Having been in development for over a year, and tested at the public beta stage by a horde of artists, the resulting application is very user-friendly, and makes common tasks such as rendering Ambient Occlusion that respects transparency – or creating render passes – a simpler prospect. It's aimed at small and large productions alike, freelancers, boutiques and small studios on tight budgets and deadlines that can't develop their own in-house pipeline solutions stand to benefit the most.

To illustrate how easy this plug-in makes rendering with AO that detects transparency, you simply enable a check box. AO for objects through several layers of transparent objects is supported by adjusting a depth slider. Traditional workarounds for this simple yet key feature are difficult to achieve, and are

the subject of many forum posts. To create render passes, you just select the passes you want from a list and move them into the Scene Passes window. Here they can be render-previewed, which is great from a production standpoint for reducing guesswork, before being sent to the Associated Passes window for batch rendering. Presets, custom Presets and Linking options are also readily available.

The plug-in includes a well-documented Shader Library that contains a variety of custom core materials such as a universal Shader called core material. It's basically a hybrid of Maya Shaders and mental ray's architectural Shader. For subsurface scattering, the core skin SSS or core simple SSS can be used with the core material. Preview rendering the subsurface pass makes tweaking hassle-free. Other core materials include a mia material, hair, car paint, blend materials and surface shader. Custom Texture Shaders and lighting Shaders are also available. Other features include a Python API to assist pipeline integration, Linear,

sRGB and Rec 709 colour management, light bloom for glow, environment lighting for ambient lighting and camera features such as colour grading and tone mapping. Video tutorials are available via the CoreCG website to help you get started, but accompanying scene files are unfortunately not available.

Suffice to say that with any new software, some minor bugs can be expected. During testing, developer Corey Frew provided an update patch for me to try that fixed a couple of problems (which I hadn't encountered) with version 1.0. This caused instability, so Corey provided a work-in-progress pre-release version of 1.1 to try. So the 1.1 update is on the way, potentially by the time you read this review, to fix known bugs. The update is also planned to introduce mental ray Standalone and Satellite support, which is lacking in version 1.0.

If you're using mental ray and in the market for a time-saving tool with plenty of features and a dedicated developer to back it up, MentalCore delivers. ●

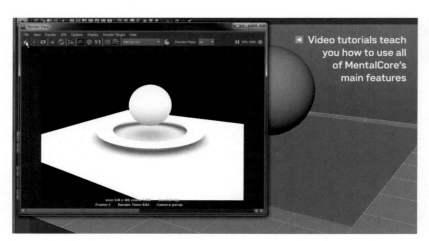

■ Video tutorials teach you how to use all of MentalCore's main features

About the author
Paul Champion is the demonstrator for undergraduate and postgraduate 3D and VFX courses at the National Centre for Computer Animation, Bournemouth

3D VERDICT

PROS
• Enhances mental ray
• Developed for production needs
• Easy to use

CONS
• Satellite rendering unsupported
• Standalone unsupported
• Tutorials lack scene files

MentalCore resolves common render workflow problems and puts mental ray integration on another, better level

Workstations for Professionals...

NVIDIA® Maximus™ Technology - Create without the Wait.

With an NVIDIA Maximus powered workstation from , you can create photorealistic renders up to 9x faster and obtain almost 6x better price/for video encoding – while simultaneously working in your primary design application. With NVIDIA Maximus technology companies no longer have to create workflows with multiple stages or on separate systems to combine the power of visual computing with high-performance computing. The combination of NVIDIA® Quadro® and Tesla GPUs allow the Tesla co-processors to automatically take the heavy lifting of rendering, freeing the Quadro GPUs to do what they do best, enabling rich interactive graphics. So you can do it all – all at the same time.

Desktop Workstations

3D Design, Visualisation, Analysis/Simulation, Post-Production, Rendering, and more...

- Powerful 12x Core System Architecture
- Triple/Quad Channel Memory (Max 192GB)
- Solid State Hard Disk Drives (up to 600GB)
- NVIDIA® Quadro™ Professional 3D Graphics
- NVIDIA® Maximus™ GPU Technology
- Perfect for Complex 3D VFX Workflows
- Bespoke Configuration for ANY Project/Budget

Maximus Performance for **3ds Max 2012** with iray[1]

Fast, Fluid editing with **Premier Pro**

*Prices from £3.48 p/day

Workstation Specialists

NVIDIA MAXIMUS TECHNOLOGY

+44 (0) 800 180 4801   sales@**wks**mail.com   www.**workstation**specialists.com

Software
VFX plug-in

PRICE
$499
Upgrade from $99

OTHER EDITIONS
Autodesk, Avid, Final Cut, Nuke, OFX; prices from $499
Theme packs with fewer effects are available; prices from $99

PLATFORM
Windows / Mac OS X

MAIN FEATURES
- Natural phenomena such as Rain, Snow and Sky
- Particles, Smoke and Sparkles
- Time-based trails and blurs
- New Starfield, Candle and Water effects
- Abstract and photorealistic filters

DEVELOPER
GenArts

WEBSITE
genarts.com

◀ The strong emphasis on natural effects is showcased brilliantly by photorealistic Raindrops

Monsters GT 7 for After Effects

The new release of Monsters GT is half the price and, as **Christopher Kenworthy** reveals, it's packed with unique effects

Unlike many filters packages, which try to offer everything from colour correction to lens flares, Monsters GT 7 presents a more stylised look. These aren't filters that you'll use on every project, but when you need a unique look or a specific effect it may be found here. The effects have a similar organic quality to GenArts Sapphire Effects, but there's a stronger emphasis on natural phenomena.

Filters are now grouped into categories such as Blurs, Fluidz and Natural Phenomena, making navigation easier than before. Controls are intuitive to use, with overlays appearing on screen to show how your changes are affecting the filter's parameters. Render times are quite slow, meaning that you may have to work at a lower resolution and then bump it up to full res for fine-tuning, depending on your system. Nothing is too sluggish to work with, though.

▶ A combination of water-based filters, including 3D Pool and Water, create realistic water effects even on 2D images

The pay-off for longer render times is usually more realism, and that's certainly the case with Monsters GT. The Natural Phenomena effects have a particularly organic feel to them, and all the water-based effects are capable of looking photorealistic with careful application.

However, some of the new features in this release are less than impressive, such as the Roman Tile effect, which does nothing more than offer another variation on crystallising the image. The Sky filter creates an instant sky complete with sun, but it has such an unrealistic look that its use may be limited.

IMPRESSIVE EFFECTS

More impressive is the new Candle effect, which creates a flickering flame that sways and drifts according to its movement. With a great depth to the controls, there's enormous scope for creative use of this effect.

Star Field, which has a 3D look and feel, can be controlled directly or automatically when you're short of time, so that stars flow around or towards the camera. The new Water effect adds subtle light waves to a surface, and works best in conjunction with other water-based filters.

Many of the particle-based filters have been improved with added motion blur and higher quality rendering. Smoke, Rain and Snow are now among the best on the market. The Raindrops filter creates a stunning impression of water dripping

down glass. 3D Pool and 3D Puddle render ripples and waves of the highest quality. The blurs and time-based effects all work effectively but don't offer major improvements over similar filters in other products. The Particles filter, however, is one of the better particle effects on the market, making it easy to create natural-looking swirls and drifts of smoky particles.

Monsters GT 7 isn't a package of must-have effects but it is a good product to have up your sleeve. When you need something that doesn't look off-the-shelf, you're more likely to find it here than in a standard package. The Natural Phenomena are the strongest offerings, with the flame, smoke, particle and water effects being some of the best you can find. ●

 **VERDICT**

PROS
- Price has been halved
- Realistic natural effects
- Many unique looks

CONS
- Some average effects
- Long render times

With original effects, organic looks and great depth of control, Monsters GT 7 provides creative control for a low price

About the author
Christopher Kenworthy is a writer and film-maker based in Australia, with a background in VFX work. He's the author of the best-selling Master Shots books christopherkenworthy.com

The smarter guide to technology.
Whichever way you look at it.

Available in print, online, on mobile and iPad

www.t3.com

The latest issue of T3 is available now at iTunes, Zinio or at all good newsagents.

▶ "We had all our animators go to 'homunculus school', where everybody worked on run, crawl and fast crawl movements," says Glenn Melenhorst. "From that we cherrypicked the best to create a movement reference bible"

Freeze Frame
Key moments in VFX and animation history revisited on DVD and Blu-ray

Little horrors

Australian studio Iloura discusses the creation of diminutive 'tooth fairy' demons for the film Don't be Afraid of the Dark. By Mark Ramshaw

▲ "Lead animator Avi Goodman came up with a rig that was economical but still with a lot of control," says Glenn Melenhorst. "We also had skin rigs to deal with folds in loose skin"

VITAL STATISTICS
Title Don't be Afraid of the Dark
Released Out now
Formats Blu-ray/DVD
Distributor Optimum Home Releasing (UK), Sony Pictures Home Entertainment (US)
Watch for... The bathroom scene, where the homunculi close in on their bathing victim and all manner of cleverly choreographed hell breaks loose

Don't be Afraid of the Dark is that rare beast – a modern horror film that's effects-heavy yet relies on old-fashioned suspense and shock tactics. But then, while it marks the directing debut of comic book illustrator Troy Nixey, it also bears the stamp of Guillermo del Toro. With the 'dark fantasy' posterboy working as scriptwriter, producer and project shepherd it's little wonder that the film transcends its roots as a schlocky 1970s TV movie to become a smart companion piece to The Devil's Backbone and Pan's Labyrinth.

The film ostensibly stars Guy Pearce, Katie Holmes and child actor Bailee Madison, but the small army of homunculi created by Australian visual effects outfit Iloura almost steals the show. "What we didn't want to do was to make Gremlins," notes visual effects director Glenn Melenhorst. "There are one or two playful scenes, but these creatures needed to possess a real sense of threat. Of course, creating scenes featuring large numbers of them helped. One mouse might look cute, but dozens of them swarming around definitely don't."

Ineke Majoor, head of VFX at Iloura, says the project ended up being the studio's biggest to date. "We handled over 300 shots, with a team of around 50 during post-production, although we were involved right through the pre-production and pre-viz process."

While the fact that the film was due to be shot near Iloura's Melbourne base was fortuitous, Majoor says they still worked hard to win the bid: "Our all-digital pig from Charlotte's Web was something of a catalyst, as both Guillermo del Toro and director Troy Nixey had seen that and liked the work, but there was still no clear indicator who it was going to be awarded to. So we also took it upon ourselves to create a test shot.

"In a one-week turnaround with a team of five, we shot a backplate, tracked it, built a shaded version of the character, and animated two homunculi – with one picking up a nail and another screaming through a crack in the wood."

Once they came on board, the Iloura team were able to work from maquettes created by Spectral Motion. These were

then retopologised and textured in ZBrush, with additional pores and wrinkles added.

"We also did some reworking on one of the homunculi, whose look referenced that of the actor playing Lord Blackwood," explains Melenhorst. "In addition to that, the creature count grew from eight all the way up to 50, so we came up with a library system for skin textures and hair that we could randomly attribute to obtain further variations."

Melenhorst says that they were able to build a lot of the fine detail into the displacement maps, keeping the poly count to a largely manageable level, although the level of detail required in key areas did make the models quite complex. "The mouth is an interesting one, particularly with the way they scream. There's a tongue in there, the epiglottis, the whole lot. We tended to have a lot of that stuff turned off, but for some shots we needed to be able to see right down their throats as well as all the crap between their teeth, and even slime hanging across various bits."

Iloura worked closely with Nixey to meticulously plan the live shoot, working

KEY TECHNOLOGY

Guillermo del Toro was inspired by the mole rat when developing the idea for the homunculi. These designs were then developed by the team at Spectral Motion, with scans of their maquettes passed over to Iloura.

"Starting with sculpting in ZBrush we then remodelled the character in 3ds Max, rigged and animated in Maya and went back to 3ds Max for rendering through V-Ray," says Glenn Melenhorst. "I don't think many people would argue that 3ds Max has the better poly tools, but conversely everyone would rather animate in Maya. Ultimately, we're not precious about what we use and have a lot of in-house tools for handling the flow of data. We even used Blender for the hair combing; it's simply better than anything else out there."

Muscle detail was sculpted in rather than driven using an independent simulation. "With these guys, it was more about sliding the skin over the bones," adds Melenhorst. "We rendered with a lot of subsurface scattering to make the full skeleton visible. It was very challenging to fine-tune, though – not only to get the right translucency and sense of frailness, but also because the shots were so dark and shadowy. The creatures are hidden for quite a lot of the time, and then in other shots you'd have a torch shining right through the skin."

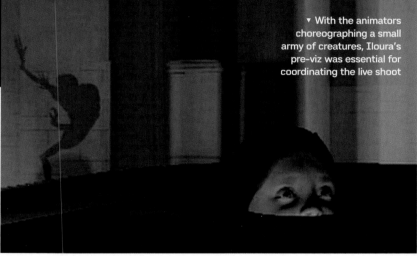

▼ With the animators choreographing a small army of creatures, Iloura's pre-viz was essential for coordinating the live shoot

▶ The first image shows the live plate, and the second shows the final digital set elements plus a group of homunculi

> *"The creature count grew from eight all the way up to 50, so we came up with a library system for skin textures and hair"*
> **Glenn Melenhorst, VFX director**

out what set elements, including floors and walls, would need removing in order to allow the camera to access the tight spaces the homunculi lurk in. "Doing pre-viz for scenes – sometimes just a couple of days prior to shooting – meant we were able to help get really involved in the design of the sequences," says Melenhorst.

"In addition to reconstructing the set with millimetre accuracy, we also built accurate digital camera rigs and booms so that everybody understood what could and couldn't happen on set, and what CG elements would be needed for shots where we wanted to do things like fly the camera amongst table legs," he adds. "We also took pains to make sure we had accurate scene, lens and focusing information. In this film, a lot of the drama comes from a creature suddenly coming out of the shadows or into focus."

Post-production gains

Melenhorst says that working so closely with the production team on-set paid dividends when it came to post-production. "Although the pre-viz wasn't completely verbatim, it provided a good grounding when it came to tracking the footage. And of course we'd been able to take all the HDRI we needed, which gave us a good starting point for our lighting setups."

In addition to working closely with the director during the shoot, Melenhorst says that del Toro also provided a guiding hand in the visual effects. He was based in New Zealand – prepping for his planned directorial work on The Hobbit – so the Iloura team were able to travel back and forth to get direct feedback on work in progress.

"We're used to working closely with an overall supervisor, but in this project we had a very direct line," says Melenhorst. "I was working as the VFX supervisor and also as part of the team, which meant we were really able to get involved creatively – not just bringing the filmmakers' vision to life but also enhancing it. They really trusted us to do what we do. It was a great collaboration." ●

Class dismissed

Roy may think that he's too cool for school, but even he has some sympathy for students struggling to choose the right animation course

Students, eh? Young, carefree, work-shy people who choose to fritter away their parents' money, run up unimaginable debts that will take 20 years to repay and do untold damage to their liver (ostensibly in pursuit of a degree, but more pressingly to gain VIP access to three years' worth of partying and to finally get laid) come in for a lot of stick from those of us who actually have to work for a living. But even I have to grudgingly admit that narrowing down exactly what to study and where isn't easy for those misguided enough to pursue a career in animation or visual effects.

Choose the wrong marine biology course and who's going to notice? It's not as if there are any job openings for marine biologists anyway. You may as well have spent three years wearing a snorkel and perfecting your Jacques Cousteau impression for all the help it'll be securing a job after graduation. The same goes for pretty much any media studies course. Even the tutors peddling those things know that studying the media doesn't actually lead to a career *in* the media. It just means that while you're sat at home, unemployed and wearing your dressing gown all day, you can waffle on like some smartarse while the

About the author
Mental Roy has been lurking on the fringes of the 3D industry for years – usually fringes that contain pubs. We could tell you his real name, but then we'd have to kill you… 3dworldmag.com

parents who funded your whole sorry degree course try in vain to watch their soap operas in peace.

It's a different story for crayon-wielders, where the gulf between the right animation course and the wrong one can be as large as the difference in quality between Finding Nemo and Cars 2. (Well, maybe not quite *that* big.) Get it right and, after graduation, you could find yourself immersed in deep shadows, shacked up with the industry's finest in New Zealand. Get it wrong and you could find yourself immersed in an outsourcing shack somewhere.

If you're lucky enough to be accepted by a high-flying talent hothouse such as Ringling, Filmakademie or Gobelins, then you're sorted, obviously. Hell, you won't even have to show up for any of the classes. Simply drop the name of your esteemed palace of higher learning at the job interview and you'll immediately get a foot in the door, a salary that needs to be expressed exponentially, and your arse in the visual effects director's hotseat... at least until your proud new employers discover that you can't even string two blendshapes together.

But spare a thought for the mere mortals who have to pore over prospectuses and college websites laced with hyperbole, course jargon and shameless marketing bollocks in a desperate bid to avoid entrusting their career prospects to an underfunded and oversold course run from a crumbling and underequipped building by a half-blind, fully alcoholic tutor whose last brush with the animation industry took place when buying shares in Silicon Graphics still seemed like a good idea...

Degree courses in Motion Graphics *and* Animation? That's a year and a half wasted mucking about with screen wipes and dissolves, for a start. A course in 3D Animation and Web Design? Since when did these two skills have anything whatsoever to do with each other? A course that covers "time-based concept origination"? Do me a favour. How long does it take to look up the word 'deadline' in the dictionary, exactly? "Opportunities to engage with the industry"? That'll be an occasional visit from a reluctant, down-on-his-

Get it right and, after graduation, you could be shacked up with the industry's finest in New Zealand

luck VFX supervisor well-versed in the art of rolling his eyes and muttering profanities under his breath. A "broad, general education in the theory and practice of computer-generated animation"? Does the phrase 'jack of all trades, master of none' ring any bells? And as for "the opportunity to work with cutting-edge animation technology", could they be referring to a room with a few standard desktop PCs running Maya, by any chance?

In truth, it doesn't take Sherlock Holmes' powers of deduction to know that all that really matters is that your chosen course has already spawned a bunch of graduates who now work at all the cool studios. A decent education doesn't harm any, but it's the old boys' network that really counts.

Besides, if all else fails, it's not as if you can't put all those newly learned, badly taught skills to use elsewhere. Remember: those who can, do. Those who can't, teach. And for those who can't but are pretty good at lying, there's always journalism. ●

3D WORLD

On the disc
Essential assets and training for every 3D artist

3D WORLD
DISC 154
3dworldmag.com

Tasty renders
Discover V-Ray 2.0 with tutorials by Chaos Group

Free textures
29 surface textures with multiple maps from Photosculpt

Video help
Expert training for ZBrush, Blender and After Effects

109 minutes of video on the disc, including a V-Ray 2.0 special! Plus: texture sampler

Assets from third-party providers are not available to readers of 3D World digital editions, but all readers are eligible for any 3D World reader offers and this issue's tutorial files

recycle
Respect the Environment
Throwing away old or surplus discs?
If you would like your Discs to be recycled rather than put into landfill, please post them to:
Polymer-Reprocessors,
Reeds Lane, Moreton, Wirral, CH46 1DW
Please respect the environment and dispose of waste plastic responsibly.

Tutorial files
Where to find the scene files you need this issue

Apart from the training videos on the disc (see opposite page), all remaining videos and scene files for this issue's tutorials are provided for free on the 3D World website. Just visit **3dworldmag.com/154**

Having problems?
If you have problems using the disc interface, visit our support website at **www.futureplc.com/disc-support**. On this regularly updated site, you'll find solutions to many commonly reported problems. If you're still experiencing problems, email our support team at **support@futurenet.com**. If you have a broken or faulty disc, return it to the address on the back of the disc wallet.

Video guide
46 minutes of hints and tips for V-Ray 2.0

VIDEO COLLECTION
Discover V-Ray 2.0
Explore the leading render engine with guides and tutorials

When achieving the ultimate in realism matters, many CG artists and visualisers turn to V-Ray, the acclaimed rendering system from Chaos Group with versions available for 3ds Max, Maya, SketchUp and Rhino. (V-Ray for Softimage is coming soon.) Currently released for 3ds Max and Maya, V-Ray 2.0 extends the system's potential even further, with major enhancements to graphics card support to boost real-time rendering, new materials including hair & fur and car paint, and the VRayLightSelect render element.

V-Ray developer Chaos Group has provided 3D World readers with videos showcasing all of these features and more, helping you explore the new tools at your disposal in V-Ray 2.0. There are over 46 minutes of V-Ray 2.0 guides and tutorials on the disc.

WEBSITE chaosgroup.com

Photosculpt Textures 2 sampler

29 high-res surfaces created with Photosculpt Textures

Photosculpt Textures 2 enables you to create tileable high-res textures from your own photos. The software is free for non-commercial use. The disc includes a sampler of 29 textures made with the software: each 2,048x2,048 set includes diffuse, bump, AO, displacement and normal maps.

FORMAT JPEG
LICENCE Commercial

WEBSITE photosculpt.net

ZBrush video training

Find out how to convert a DynaMesh sculpture

In this issue's Q&A section, starting on page 96, Glen Southern explains how to convert a sculpture made with ZBrush's DynaMesh toolset so that it's ready to use in other 3D packages. The disc includes a 32-minute video that adds more detail to Glen's Q&A.

Hand model video training

Watch as Mike Griggs shows you how to construct a hand

In this issue's Fundamentals on page 88, Mike Griggs explains the principles and techniques behind modelling a hand, one of the most challenging parts on any human figure. His video on the disc shows the full procedure, with the use of tools that apply to any hard-surface modelling toolset.

Blender video training

Use splines to control bones in your animation rig

In this issue's Q&A section, starting on page 96, Alex Telford explains how to use the spline-based rigging method in your Blender animations – perfect for bendy arms and other cartoony movements. Alex's 16-minute video on the disc takes you through the whole procedure in more detail, and scene files are available via **3dworldmag.com/154**.

After Effects video training

Bite-sized guide to spray-paint reveals

In this issue's Q&A section, starting on page 96, Tom Skelton shows you how to enliven your final video edit with a reveal between cuts, with the help of an animated stroke-based transition. Tom's video on the disc shows how you can apply the technique in a little over three-and-a-half minutes. Try it out, then create your own variations.

On your free disc

Explore your disc
If the disc does not run automatically, double-click the 3DW.osx or 3DW.exe icon to launch the interface

THIS ISSUE Video tutorials on rendering with V-Ray 2.0 from Chaos Group, Photosculpt high-resolution textures pack plus exclusive video training

Videos

V-Ray 2.0
46 minutes of video on the leading render system from Chaos Group

Resources

Photosculpt texture sampler
With 29 free high-resolution textures including diffuse, bump, displacement, AO and normal maps

Tutorial files

Fundamentals video
How to model a hand from scratch with our exclusive video

Q&A videos
Extend your ZBrush, Blender and After Effects skills with our video tutorials

Visit **3dworldmag.com/154** for all the remaining scene files and videos relating to this issue's expert tutorials.

The disc interface for this disc is not compatible with Mac OS X Lion: please locate files via the Finder

Is your disc missing?
Please consult your newsagent, then contact us to obtain a replacement
support@futurenet.com

For a full listing of our disc content this issue, including file formats and system requirements, **turn to page 112**

Respect the Environment
Throwing away old or surplus discs?
If you would like your Discs to be recycled rather than put into landfill, please post them to:
Polymer-Reprocessors,
Reeds Lane, Moreton, Wirral, CH46 1DW
Please respect the environment and dispose of waste plastic responsibly.

In the next 3D World:
Fund your dream 3D movie • John Carter of Mars • Heroic characters
UK stores, Newsstand & Zinio **27 Mar** • US & Canada stores **24 Apr**